LIFE AND DEATH

IN A VENETIAN CONVENT

THE
OTHER VOICE
IN
EARLY MODERN
EUROPE

A Series Edited by Margaret L. King and Albert Rabil, Jr.

Sister Bartolomea Riccoboni

LIFE AND DEATH
IN A VENETIAN CONVENT:
THE CHRONICLE AND
NECROLOGY OF CORPUS
DOMINI, 1395 – 1436

ꝫ

Edited and Translated
by
Daniel Bornstein

THE UNIVERSITY OF CHICAGO PRESS
Chicago & London

Daniel Bornstein is professor of history at Texas A&M University.

The University of Chicago Press, Chicago 60637
The University of Chicago Press, Ltd., London
© 2000 by The University of Chicago
All rights reserved. Published 2000
09 08 07 06 05 04 03 02 01 00   1 2 3 4 5

ISBN: 0-226-71788-7 (cloth)
ISBN: 0-226-71789-5 (paper)

Library of Congress Cataloging-in-Publication Data

Riccoboni, Bartolomea, 14th /15th cent.
    Life and death in a Venetian convent : the chronicle and necrology
of Corpus Domini, 1395–1436 / Bartolomea Riccoboni ; edited and
translated by Daniel Bornstein.
        p.   cm. — (The other voice in early modern Europe)
    Includes bibliographical references and index.
    ISBN 0-226-71788-7 (alk. paper). — ISBN 0-226-71789-5 (pbk. : alk. paper)
    1. Corpus Domini (Convent : Venice, Italy)—History.   2. Dominican
Nuns of the Second Order of Perpetual Adoration Necrology.
3. Venice (Italy)—Church history.   I. Bornstein, Daniel Ethan,
1950–   . II. Title.   III. Series.
BX4337.5.V46R53   2000
271′.97204531—dc21   99-37584
                                                                      CIP

CONTENTS

PREFACE

In the course of preparing this translation I have often (like Sister Bartolomea) been acutely conscious "of my inadequacy, since such an undertaking requires wise and learned persons." Luckily, I have enjoyed the support of
a number of institutions and individuals who have generously offered me their
wisdom and helped to mitigate my ignorance. The translation was prepared
with the support of a Faculty Development Leave from Texas A&M University
and a National Endowment for the Humanities Fellowship at the Newberry
Library, Chicago. A fellowship from the Gladys Krieble Delmas Foundation, a grant-in-aid from the American Philosophical Society, and a Faculty
Research Fellowship from the Program in Women's Studies of Texas A&M
University made possible a summer of archival research in Venice and the
preparation of the introduction and annotation to the texts. In Venice itself,
the staffs of the Archivio di Stato and of the Biblioteca del Museo Correr made
their manuscript collections available with unfailing courtesy and admirable
professionalism. Laura C. Bornstein, Maria Cristina Garcia, and the students
in my senior seminar on Saints and Society (fall 1995) offered a number of
helpful comments on an early draft of the translation; the students in another
seminar, on Women and Religion in Medieval Europe (spring 1998), scruti-
nized a more polished translation, as well as the introduction and annotation.
Jane Bornstein did double (or triple) duty, reading each draft in turn; Roberto
Rusconi helped unravel some obscure passages in the texts; and John Martin
gave me the benefit of his expert knowledge of Renaissance Venice. And when
I thought I finally had it right, Margaret L. King and Albert Rabil Jr. pressed me
to rethink and recast the introduction and offered cogent and helpful advice
on how to do so.

A special, and immense, debt of gratitude is owed to the long and distinguished tradition of Venetian scholarship. Again and again I have turned for

guidance to Giuseppe Boerio's *Dizionario del dialetto veneziano,* so attentive to nuance and rich in examples and cross-references. I have relied on and marveled at the erudition of Flaminio Corner and Giovanni degli Agostini, learned contemporaries of the great Ludovico Antonio Muratori, whose mastery of Venice's libraries and archives is matched by few modern scholars. And I have learned much, and continue to learn, from the Paduan school of Paolo Sambin, Giorgio Cracco, and Antonio Rigon. Over a decade ago, one young member of that school, Maria Ricci, gave a copy of her excellent *tesi di laurea* on the convent of Corpus Domini to an American scholar she had never met; every time I consult it, as I did so often in the course of preparing this edition, I am struck by a philological rigor that matches her remarkable generosity— both, miraculously, entirely typical of the school where she trained. To the many members of this uncloistered and far-flung community of scholarship, I offer my thanks and this volume.

THE OTHER VOICE IN EARLY MODERN EUROPE: INTRODUCTION TO THE SERIES

Margaret L. King and Albert Rabil Jr.

THE OLD VOICE AND THE OTHER VOICE

In western Europe and the United States women are nearing equality in the professions, in business, and in politics. Most enjoy access to education, reproductive rights, and autonomy in financial affairs. Issues vital to women are on the public agenda: equal pay, child care, domestic abuse, breast cancer research, and curricular revision with an eye to the inclusion of women.

These recent achievements have their origins in things women (and some male supporters) said for the first time about six hundred years ago. Theirs is the "other voice," in contradistinction to the "first voice," the voice of the educated men who created Western culture. Coincident with a general reshaping of European culture in the period 1300–1700 (called the Renaissance or early modern period), questions of female equality and opportunity were raised that still resound and are still unresolved.

The "other voice" emerged against the backdrop of a three-thousand-year history of the derogation of women rooted in the civilizations related to Western culture: Hebrew, Greek, Roman, and Christian. Negative attitudes toward women inherited from these traditions pervaded the intellectual, medical, legal, religious, and social systems that developed during the European Middle Ages.

The following pages describe the traditional, overwhelmingly male views of women's nature inherited by early modern Europeans and the new tradition that the "other voice" called into being to challenge reigning assumptions. This review should serve as a framework for understanding the texts published in the series "The Other Voice in Early Modern Europe." Introductions specific to each text and author follow this essay in all the volumes of the series.

TRADITIONAL VIEWS OF WOMEN, 500 B.C.E. – 1500 C.E.

Embedded in the philosophical and medical theories of the ancient Greeks were perceptions of the female as inferior to the male in both mind and body. Similarly, the structure of civil legislation inherited from the ancient Romans was biased against women, and the views on women developed by Christian thinkers out of the Hebrew Bible and the Christian New Testament were negative and disabling. Literary works composed in the vernacular of ordinary people, and widely recited or read, conveyed these negative assumptions. The social networks within which most women lived—those of the family and the institutions of the Roman Catholic Church—were shaped by this negative tradition and sharply limited the areas in which women might act in and upon the world.

GREEK PHILOSOPHY AND FEMALE NATURE. Greek biology assumed that women were inferior to men and defined them as merely childbearers and housekeepers. This view was authoritatively expressed in the works of the philosopher Aristotle.

Aristotle thought in dualities. He considered action superior to inaction, form (the inner design or structure of any object) superior to matter, completion to incompletion, possession to deprivation. In each of these dualities he associated the male principle with the superior quality and the female with the inferior. "The male principle in nature," he argued, "is associated with active, formative and perfected characteristics, while the female is passive, material and deprived, desiring the male in order to become complete."[1] Men are always identified with virile qualities, such as judgment, courage, and stamina, and women with their opposites—irrationality, cowardice, and weakness.

The masculine principle was considered to be superior even in the womb. The man's semen, Aristotle believed, created the form of a new human creature, while the female body contributed only matter. (The existence of the ovum, and the other facts of human embryology, was not established until the seventeenth century.) Although the later Greek physician Galen believed there was a female component in generation, contributed by "female semen," the followers of both Aristotle and Galen saw the male role in human generation as more active and more important.

In the Aristotelian view, the male principle sought to reproduce itself. The creation of a female was always a mistake, therefore, resulting from an imperfect act of generation. Every female born was considered a "defective" or

---

1. Aristotle, *Physics* 1.9 192a20–24 (Barnes, 1.328).

"mutilated" male (as Aristotle's terminology has variously been translated), a "monstrosity" of nature.[2]

For Greek theorists, the biology of males and females was the key to their psychology. The female was softer and more docile, more apt to be despondent, querulous, and deceitful. Being incomplete, moreover, she craved sexual fulfillment in intercourse with a male. The male was intellectual, active, and in control of his passions.

These psychological polarities derived from the theory that the universe consisted of four elements (earth, fire, air, and water), expressed in human bodies as four "humors" (black bile, yellow bile, blood, and phlegm) considered respectively dry, hot, damp, and cold, and corresponding to mental states ("melancholic," "choleric," "sanguine," "phlegmatic"). In this scheme the male, sharing the principles of earth and fire, was dry and hot; the female, sharing the principles of air and water, was damp and cold.

Woman's psychology was further affected by her dominant organ, the uterus (womb), *hystera* in Greek. The passions generated by the womb made women lustful, deceitful, talkative, irrational, indeed—when these affects were in excess—"hysterical."

Aristotle's biology also had social and political consequences. If the male principle was superior and the female inferior, then in the household, as in the state, men should govern and women must be subordinate. That hierarchy did not rule out the companionship of husband and wife, whose cooperation was necessary for the welfare of children and the preservation of property. Such mutuality supported male preeminence.

Aristotle's teacher Plato suggested a different possibility: that men and women might possess the same virtues. The setting for this proposal is the imaginary and ideal Republic that Plato sketches in his dialogue of that name. Here, for a privileged elite capable of leading wisely, all distinctions of class and wealth dissolve, as consequently do those of gender. Without households or property, as Plato constructs his ideal society, there is no need for the subordination of women. Women may therefore be educated to the same level as men to assume leadership. Plato's Republic remained imaginary, however. In real societies, the subordination of women remained the norm and the prescription.

The views of women inherited from the Greek philosophical tradition became the basis for medieval thought. In the thirteenth century the supreme Scholastic philosopher Thomas Aquinas, among others, still echoed Aristo-

---

2. Aristotle, *Generation of Animals* 2.3 737a27–28 (*The Complete Works of Aristotle*, ed. Jonathan Barnes, rev. Oxford translation, 2 vols. [Princeton, 1984], 1.1144).

tle's views of human reproduction, of male and female personalities, and of the preeminent role of the male in the social hierarchy.

ROMAN LAW AND THE FEMALE CONDITION. Roman law, like Greek philosophy, underlay medieval thought and shaped medieval society. The ancient belief that adult, property-owning men should administer households and make decisions affecting the community at large is the very fulcrum of Roman law.

About 450 B.C.E., during Rome's republican era, the community's customary law was recorded (legendarily) on twelve tables erected in the city's central forum. It was later elaborated by professional jurists whose activity increased in the imperial era, when much new legislation was passed, especially on issues affecting family and inheritance. This growing, changing body of laws was eventually codified in the *Corpus of Civil Law* under the direction of the emperor Justinian, generations after the empire ceased to be ruled from Rome. That *Corpus*, read and commented on by medieval scholars from the eleventh century on, inspired the legal systems of most of the cities and kingdoms of Europe.

Laws regarding dowries, divorce, and inheritance mostly pertain to women. Since those laws aimed to maintain and preserve property, the women concerned were those from the property-owning minority. Their subordination to male family members points to the even greater subordination of lower-class and slave women, about whom the laws speak little.

In the early republic the *paterfamilias*, "father of the family," possessed *patria potestas*, "paternal power." The term *pater*, "father," in both these cases does not necessarily mean biological father but denotes a householder. The father was the person who owned the household's property and, indeed, its human members. The *paterfamilias* had absolute power—including the power, rarely exercised, of life or death—over his wife, his children, and his slaves as much as his cattle.

Male children could be "emancipated," an act that granted them legal autonomy and the right to own property. Those over fourteen could be emancipated by a special grant from the father, or automatically by the father's death. But females could never be emancipated; instead, they passed from the authority of the father to that of a husband or, if widowed or orphaned while still unmarried, a guardian or tutor.

Marriage in its traditional form placed the woman under her husband's authority, or *manus*. He could divorce her on grounds of adultery, drinking wine, or stealing from the household, but she could not divorce him. She could possess no property in her own right, nor could she bequeath any to her children upon her death. When her husband died the household property passed not to her but to his male heirs. And when her father died she had no claim to any family inheritance, which was directed to her brothers or more remote male relatives. The effect of these laws was to exclude women from civil society, itself based on property ownership.

In the later republican and imperial periods these rules were significantly modified, and women rarely married according to the traditional form. The practice of "free" marriage allowed a woman to remain under her father's authority, to possess property given to her by her father (most frequently the "dowry," recoverable from the husband's household on his death), and to inherit from her father. She could also bequeath property to her own children and divorce her husband, just as he could divorce her.

Despite this greater freedom, women still suffered enormous disability under Roman law. Heirs could belong only to the father's side, never the mother's. Moreover, although she could bequeath her property to her children, she could not establish a line of succession in doing so. A woman was "the beginning and end of her own family," said the jurist Ulpian. Moreover, women could play no public role. They could not hold public office, represent anyone in a legal case, or even witness a will. Women had only a private existence and no public personality.

The dowry system, the guardian, women's limited ability to transmit wealth, and their total political disability are all features of Roman law adopted by the medieval communities of western Europe, although modified according to local customary laws.

CHRISTIAN DOCTRINE AND WOMEN'S PLACE. The Hebrew Bible and the Christian New Testament authorized later writers to limit women to the realm of the family and to burden them with the guilt of original sin. The passages most fruitful for this purpose were the creation narratives in Genesis and sentences from the Epistles defining women's role within the Christian family and community.

Each of the first two chapters of Genesis contains a creation narrative. In the first "God created man in his own image, in the image of God he created him; male and female he created them" (Gen. 1:27). In the second, God created Eve from Adam's rib (2:21–23). Christian theologians relied principally on Genesis 2 for their understanding of the relationship between man and woman, interpreting the creation of Eve from Adam as proof of her subordination to him.

The creation story in Genesis 2 leads to that of the temptations in Genesis 3: of Eve by the wily serpent and of Adam by Eve. As read by Christian theologians from Tertullian to Thomas Aquinas, the narrative made Eve responsible for the Fall and its consequences. She instigated the act; she deceived her husband; she suffered the greater punishment. Her disobedience made it necessary for Jesus to be incarnated and to die on the cross. From the pulpit, moralists and preachers for centuries conveyed to women the guilt they bore for original sin.

The Epistles offered advice to early Christians on building communities of the faithful. Among the matters to be regulated was the place of women. Paul offered views favorable to women in Gal. 3:28: "There is neither Jew nor Greek, there is neither slave nor free, there is neither male nor female; for you are all one in Christ Jesus." Paul also referred to women as his coworkers and placed them on a par with himself and his male coworkers (Phil. 4:2–3; Rom. 16:1–3; 1 Cor. 16:19). Elsewhere Paul limited women's possibilities: "But I want you to understand that the head of every man is Christ, the head of a woman is her husband, and the head of Christ is God" (1 Cor. 11:3).

Biblical passages by later writers (though attributed to Paul) enjoined women to forgo jewels, expensive clothes, and elaborate coiffures; and they forbade women to "teach or have authority over men," telling them to "learn in silence with all submissiveness" as is proper for one responsible for sin, consoling them however with the thought that they will be saved through childbearing (1 Tim. 2:9–15). Other texts among the later Epistles defined women as the weaker sex and emphasized their subordination to their husbands (1 Peter 3:7; Col. 3:18; Eph. 5:22–23).

These passages from the New Testament became the arsenal employed by theologians of the early church to transmit negative attitudes toward women to medieval Christian culture—above all, Tertullian ("On the Apparel of Women"), Jerome (*Against Jovinian*), and Augustine (*The Literal Meaning of Genesis*).

THE IMAGE OF WOMEN IN MEDIEVAL LITERATURE. The philosophical, legal, and religious traditions born in antiquity formed the basis of the medieval intellectual synthesis wrought by trained thinkers, mostly clerics, writing in Latin and based largely in universities. The vernacular literary tradition that developed alongside the learned tradition also spoke about female nature and women's roles. Medieval stories, poems, and epics also portrayed women negatively—as lustful and deceitful—while praising good housekeepers and loyal wives as replicas of the Virgin Mary or the female saints and martyrs.

There is an exception in the movement of "courtly love" that evolved in southern France from the twelfth century. Courtly love was erotic love between a nobleman and noblewoman, the latter usually superior in social rank. It was always adulterous. From the conventions of courtly love derive modern Western notions of romantic love. The tradition has had an impact disproportionate to its size, for it affected only a tiny elite, and very few women. The exaltation of the female lover probably does not reflect a higher evaluation of women, or a step toward their sexual liberation. More likely it gives expression to the social and sexual tensions besetting the knightly class at a specific historical juncture.

The literary fashion of courtly love was on the wane by the thirteenth century, when the widely read *Romance of the Rose* was composed in French by two authors of significantly different dispositions. Guillaume de Lorris composed the initial four thousand verses about 1235, and Jean de Meun added about seventeen thousand verses—more than four times the original—about 1265.

The fragment composed by Guillaume de Lorris stands squarely in the tradition of courtly love. Here the poet, in a dream, is admitted into a walled garden where he finds a magic fountain in which a rosebush is reflected. He longs to pick one rose, but the thorns prevent it, even as he is wounded by arrows from the god of love, whose commands he agrees to obey. The rest of this part of the poem recounts the poet's unsuccessful efforts to pluck the rose.

The longer part of the *Romance* by Jean de Meun also describes a dream. But here allegorical characters give long didactic speeches, providing a social satire on a variety of themes, some pertaining to women. Love is an anxious and tormented state, the poem explains; women are greedy and manipulative, marriage is miserable, beautiful women are lustful, ugly ones cease to please, and a chaste woman is as rare as a black swan.

Shortly after Jean de Meun completed *The Romance of the Rose*, Mathéolus penned his *Lamentations*, a long Latin diatribe against marriage translated into French about a century later. The *Lamentations* summed up medieval attitudes toward women and provoked the important response by Christine de Pizan in her *Book of the City of Ladies*.

In 1355 Giovanni Boccaccio wrote *Il corbaccio*, another antifeminist manifesto, though ironically by an author whose other works pioneered new directions in Renaissance thought. The former husband of his lover appears to Boccaccio, condemning his unmoderated lust and detailing the defects of women. Boccaccio concedes at the end "how much men naturally surpass women in nobility"[3] and is cured of his desires.

WOMEN'S ROLES: THE FAMILY. The negative perception of women expressed in the intellectual tradition is also implicit in the actual roles women played in European society. Assigned to subordinate positions in the house-

---

3. Giovanni Boccaccio, *The Corbaccio, or The Labyrinth of Love*, trans. and ed. Anthony K. Cassell (Binghamton, N.Y., rev. paper ed., 1993), 71.

hold and the church, they were barred from significant participation in public life.

Medieval European households, like those in antiquity and in non-Western civilizations, were headed by males. It was the male serf, peasant, feudal lord, town merchant, or citizen who was polled or taxed or succeeded to an inheritance or had any acknowledged public role, although his wife or widow could stand as a temporary surrogate for him. From about 1100, the position of property-holding males was further enhanced. Inheritance was confined to the male, or agnate, line—with depressing consequences for women.

A wife never fully belonged to her husband's family nor a daughter to her father's. She left her father's house young to marry whomever her parents chose. Her dowry was managed by her husband, and at her death it normally passed to her children by him.

A married woman's life was occupied nearly constantly with cycles of pregnancy, childbearing, and lactation. Women bore children through all the years of their fertility, and many died in childbirth. They also were responsible for raising young children up to six or seven. In the propertied classes that responsibility was shared, since it was common for a wet nurse to take over breast-feeding, and servants performed other chores.

Women trained their daughters in the household duties appropriate to their status, nearly always tasks associated with textiles: spinning, weaving, sewing, embroidering. Their sons were sent out of the house as apprentices or students, or their fathers assumed their training in later childhood and adolescence. On the death of her husband, a woman's children became the responsibility of his family. She generally did not take "his" children with her to a new marriage or back to her father's house, except sometimes in artisan classes.

Women also worked. Peasants performed farm chores, merchant wives often practiced their husbands' trades, the unmarried daughters of the urban poor worked as servants or prostitutes. All wives produced or embellished textiles and did the housekeeping, and wealthy ones managed servants. These labors were unpaid or poorly paid but often contributed substantially to family wealth.

WOMEN'S ROLES: THE CHURCH. Membership in a household, whether a father's or a husband's, meant for women a lifelong subordination to others. In western Europe the Roman Catholic Church offered an alternative to the career of wife and mother. A woman could enter a convent parallel in function to the monasteries for men that evolved in the early Christian centuries.

In the convent, a woman pledged herself to a celibate life, lived according to strict community rules, and worshiped daily. Often the convent offered training in Latin, allowing some women to become considerable scholars and authors as well as scribes, artists, and musicians. For women who chose the conventual life the benefits could be enormous, but for numerous others placed in convents by paternal choice, the life could be restrictive and burdensome.

The conventual life declined as an alternative for women as the modern age approached. Reformed monastic institutions resisted responsibility for related female orders. The church increasingly restricted female institutional life by insisting on closer male supervision.

Women often sought other options. Some joined the communities of laywomen that sprang up spontaneously in the thirteenth century in the urban zones of western Europe, especially in Flanders and Italy. Some joined the heretical movements that flourished in late medieval Christendom, whose anticlerical and often antifamily positions particularly appealed to women. In these communities some women were acclaimed as "holy women" or "saints," whereas others often were condemned as frauds or heretics.

Though the options offered to women by the church were sometimes less than satisfactory, they were sometimes richly rewarding. After 1520 the convent remained an option only in Roman Catholic territories. Protestantism engendered an ideal of marriage as a heroic endeavor and appeared to place husband and wife on a more equal footing. Sermons and treatises, however, still called for female subordination and obedience.

THE OTHER VOICE, 1300 – 1700

When the modern era opened, European culture was so firmly structured by a framework of negative attitudes toward women that to dismantle it was a monumental labor. The process began as part of a larger cultural movement that entailed the critical reexamination of ideas inherited from the ancient and medieval past. The humanists launched that critical reexamination.

THE HUMANIST FOUNDATION. Originating in Italy in the fourteenth century, humanism quickly became the dominant intellectual movement in Europe. Spreading in the sixteenth century from Italy to the rest of Europe, it fueled the literary, scientific, and philosophical movements of the era and laid the basis for the eighteenth-century Enlightenment.

Humanists regarded the Scholastic philosophy of medieval universities as out of touch with the realities of urban life. They found in the rhetorical discourse of classical Rome a language adapted to civic life and public speech. They learned to read, speak, and write classical Latin, and eventually classical Greek. They founded schools to teach others to do so, establishing the pattern for elementary and secondary education for the next three hundred years.

In the service of complex government bureaucracies, humanists employed their skills to write eloquent letters, deliver public orations, and formulate public policy. They developed new scripts for copying manuscripts and used the new printing press to disseminate texts, for which they created methods of critical editing.

Humanism was a movement led by males who accepted the evaluation of women in ancient texts and generally shared the misogynist perceptions of their culture. (Female humanists, as we will see, did not.) Yet humanism also opened the door to a reevaluation of the nature and capacity of women. By calling authors, texts, and ideas into question, it made possible the fundamental rereading of the whole intellectual tradition that was required in order to free women from cultural prejudice and social subordination.

A DIFFERENT CITY. The other voice first appeared when, after so many centuries, the accumulation of misogynist concepts evoked a response from a capable female defender: Christine de Pizan (1365–1431). Introducing her *Book of the City of Ladies* (1405), she described how she was affected by reading Mathéolus's *Lamentations*: "Just the sight of this book . . . made me wonder how it happened that so many different men . . . are so inclined to express both in speaking and in their treatises and writings so many wicked insults about women and their behavior."[4] These statements impelled her to detest herself "and the entire feminine sex, as though we were monstrosities in nature."[5]

The rest of *Book of the City of Ladies* presents a justification of the female sex and a vision of an ideal community of women. A pioneer, she has received the message of female inferiority and rejected it. From the fourteenth to the seventeenth century, a huge body of literature accumulated that responded to the dominant tradition.

The result was a literary explosion consisting of works by both men and women, in Latin and in the vernaculars: works enumerating the achievements of notable women; works rebutting the main accusations made against women; works arguing for the equal education of men and women; works defining and redefining women's proper role in the family, at court, and in public; works describing women's lives and experiences. Recent monographs and articles have begun to hint at the great range of this movement, involving probably several thousand titles. The protofeminism of these "other voices" constitutes a significant fraction of the literary product of the early modern era.

4. Christine de Pizan, *Book of the City of Ladies*, trans. Earl Jeffrey Richards, foreword Marina Warner (New York, 1982), 1.1.1, pp. 3–4.
5. Ibid., 1.1.1–2, p. 5.

THE CATALOGS. About 1365, the same Boccaccio whose *Corbaccio* rehearses the usual charges against female nature wrote another work, *Concerning Famous Women*. A humanist treatise drawing on classical texts, it praised 106 notable women from pagan Greek and Roman antiquity, from the Bible (Eve), and from the medieval religious and cultural tradition; his book helped make all readers aware of a sex normally condemned or forgotten. Boccaccio's outlook nevertheless was unfriendly to women, for it singled out for praise those women who possessed the traditional virtues of chastity, silence, and obedience. Women who were active in the public realm—for example, rulers and warriors—were depicted as usually being lascivious and as suffering terrible punishments for entering the masculine sphere. Women were his subject, but Boccaccio's standard remained male.

Christine de Pizan's *Book of the City of Ladies* contains a second catalog, one responding specifically to Boccaccio's. Where Boccaccio portrays female virtue as exceptional, she depicts it as universal. Many women in history were leaders, or remained chaste despite the lascivious approaches of men, or were visionaries and brave martyrs.

The work of Boccaccio inspired a series of catalogs of illustrious women of the biblical, classical, Christian, and local pasts, among them Filippo da Bergamo's *Of Illustrious Women*, Pierre de Brantôme's *Lives of Illustrious Women*, Pierre Le Moyne's *Gallerie of Heroic Women*, and Pietro Paolo de Ribera's *Immortal Triumphs and Heroic Enterprises of 845 Women*. Whatever their embedded prejudices, these works drove home to the public the possibility of female excellence.

THE DEBATE. Yet many questions remained: Could a woman be virtuous? Could she perform noteworthy deeds? Was she even, strictly speaking, of the same human species as men? These questions were debated over four centuries, in French, German, Italian, Spanish, and English, by authors male and female, among Catholics, Protestants, and Jews, in ponderous volumes and breezy pamphlets. The whole literary genre has been called the *querelle des femmes*, the "woman question."

The opening volley of this battle occurred in the first years of the fifteenth century, in a literary debate sparked by Christine de Pizan. She exchanged letters critical of Jean de Meun's contribution to *The Romance of the Rose* with two French royal secretaries, Jean de Montreuil and Gontier Col. When the matter became public, Jean Gerson, one of Europe's leading theologians, supported her arguments against Jean de Meun, for the moment silencing the opposition.

The debate surfaced repeatedly over the next two hundred years. *The Triumph of Women* (1438) by Juan Rodríguez de la Camara (or Juan Rodríguez del

Padron) struck a new note by presenting arguments for the superiority of women to men. *The Champion of Women* (1440–42) by Martin Le Franc addresses once again the negative views of women presented in *The Romance of the Rose* and offers counterevidence of female virtue and achievement.

A cameo of the debate on women is included in *The Courtier,* one of the most widely read books of the era, published by the Italian Baldassare Castiglione in 1528 and immediately translated into other European languages. *The Courtier* depicts a series of evenings at the court of the duke of Urbino in which many men and some women of the highest social stratum amuse themselves by discussing a range of literary and social issues. The "woman question" is a pervasive theme throughout, and the third of its four books is devoted entirely to that issue.

In a verbal duel, Gasparo Pallavicino and Giuliano de' Medici present the main claims of the two traditions. Gasparo argues the innate inferiority of women and their inclination to vice. Only in bearing children do they profit the world. Giuliano counters that women share the same spiritual and mental capacities as men and may excel in wisdom and action. Men and women are of the same essence: just as no stone can be more perfectly a stone than another, so no human being can be more perfectly human than others, whether male or female. It was an astonishing assertion, boldly made to an audience as large as all Europe.

THE TREATISES. Humanism provided the materials for a positive counterconcept to the misogyny embedded in Scholastic philosophy and law and inherited from the Greek, Roman, and Christian pasts. A series of humanist treatises on marriage and family, education and deportment, and the nature of women helped construct these new perspectives.

The works by Francesco Barbaro and Leon Battista Alberti, respectively *On Marriage* (1415) and *On the Family* (1434–37), far from defending female equality, reasserted women's responsibility for rearing children and managing the housekeeping while being obedient, chaste, and silent. Nevertheless, they served the cause of reexamining the issue of women's nature by placing domestic issues at the center of scholarly concern and reopening the pertinent classical texts. In addition, Barbaro emphasized the companionate nature of marriage and the importance of a wife's spiritual and mental qualities for the well-being of the family.

These themes reappear in later humanist works on marriage and the education of women by Juan Luis Vives and Erasmus. Both were moderately sympathetic to the condition of women without reaching beyond the usual masculine prescriptions for female behavior.

An outlook more favorable to women characterizes the nearly unknown work *In Praise of Women* (ca. 1487) by the Italian humanist Bartolommeo Goggio. In addition to providing a catalog of illustrious women, Goggio argued that male and female are the same in essence, but that women (reworking the Adam and Eve narrative from quite a new angle) are actually superior. In the same vein, the Italian humanist Maria Equicola asserted the spiritual equality of men and women in *On Women* (1501). In 1525 Galeazzo Flavio Capra (or Capella) published his work *On the Excellence and Dignity of Women.* This humanist tradition of treatises defending the worthiness of women culminates in the work of Henricus Cornelius Agrippa *On the Nobility and Preeminence of the Female Sex.* No work by a male humanist more succinctly or explicitly presents the case for female dignity.

THE WITCH BOOKS. While humanists grappled with the issues pertaining to women and family, other learned men turned their attention to what they perceived as a very great problem: witches. Witch-hunting manuals, explorations of the witch phenomenon, and even defenses of witches are not at first glance pertinent to the tradition of the other voice. But they do relate in this way: most accused witches were women. The hostility aroused by supposed witch activity is comparable to the hostility aroused by women. The evil deeds the victims of the hunt were charged with were exaggerations of the vices to which, many believed, all women were prone.

The connection between the witch accusation and the hatred of women is explicit in the notorious witch-hunting manual *The Hammer of Witches* (1486), by two Dominican inquisitors, Heinrich Krämer and Jacob Sprenger. Here the inconstancy, deceitfulness, and lust traditionally associated with women are depicted in exaggerated form as the core features of witch behavior. These inclined women to make a bargain with the devil—sealed by sexual intercourse—by which they acquired unholy powers. Such bizarre claims, far from being rejected by rational men, were broadcast by intellectuals. The German Ulrich Molitur, the Frenchman Nicolas Rémy, and the Italian Stefano Guazzo coolly informed the public of sinister orgies and midnight pacts with the devil. The celebrated French jurist, historian, and political philosopher Jean Bodin argued that because women were especially prone to diabolism, regular legal procedures could properly be suspended in order to try those accused of this "exceptional crime."

A few experts, such as the physician Johann Weyer, a student of Agrippa's, raised their voices in protest. In 1563 Weyer explained the witch phenomenon thus, without discarding belief in diabolism: the devil deluded foolish old women afflicted by melancholia, causing them to believe they had magical powers. His rational skepticism, which had good credibility in the community of the learned, worked to revise the conventional views of women and witchcraft.

WOMEN'S WORKS. To the many categories of works produced on the question of women's worth must be added nearly all works written by women. A woman writing was in herself a statement of women's claim to dignity.

Only a few women wrote anything before the dawn of the modern era, for three reasons. First, they rarely received the education that would enable them to write. Second, they were not admitted to the public roles—as administrator, bureaucrat, lawyer or notary, university professor—in which they might gain knowledge of the kinds of things the literate public thought worth writing about. Third, the culture imposed silence on women, considering speaking out a form of unchastity. Given these conditions, it is remarkable that any women wrote. Those who did so before the fourteenth century were almost always nuns or religious women whose isolation made their pronouncements more acceptable.

From the fourteenth century on, the volume of women's writings rose. Women continued to write devotional literature, although not always as cloistered nuns. They also wrote diaries, often intended as keepsakes for their children; books of advice to their sons and daughters; letters to family members and friends; and family memoirs, in a few cases elaborate enough to be considered histories.

A few women wrote works directly concerning the "woman question," and some of these, such as the humanists Isotta Nogarola, Cassandra Fedele, Laura Cereta, and Olympia Morata, were highly trained. A few were professional writers, living by the income of their pens: the very first among them was Christine de Pizan, noteworthy in this context as in so many others. In addition to *Book of the City of Ladies* and her critiques of *The Romance of the Rose,* she wrote *The Treasure of the City of Ladies* (a guide to social decorum for women), an advice book for her son, much courtly verse, and a full-scale history of the reign of King Charles V of France.

WOMEN PATRONS. Women who did not themselves write but encouraged others to do so boosted the development of an alternative tradition. Highly placed women patrons supported authors, artists, musicians, poets, and learned men. Such patrons, drawn mostly from the Italian elites and the courts of northern Europe, figure disproportionately as the dedicatees of the important works of early feminism.

For a start, it might be noted that the catalogs of Boccaccio and Alvaro de Luna were dedicated to the Florentine noblewoman Andrea Acciaiuoli and to Doña María, first wife of King Juan II of Castile, while the French translation of Boccaccio's work was commissioned by Anne of Brittany, wife of King Charles VIII of France. The humanist treatises of Goggio, Equicola, Vives, and Agrippa were dedicated, respectively, to Eleanora of Aragon, wife of Ercole I d'Este, duke of Ferrara; to Margherita Cantelma of Mantua; to Catherine of Aragon, wife of King Henry VIII of England; and to Margaret, duchess of Austria and regent of the Netherlands. As late as 1696, Mary Astell's *Serious Proposal to the Ladies, for the Advancement of Their True and Greatest Interest* was dedicated to Princess Anne of Denmark.

These authors presumed that their efforts would be welcome to female patrons, or they may have written at the bidding of those patrons. Silent themselves, perhaps even unresponsive, these loftily placed women helped shape the tradition of the other voice.

THE ISSUES. The literary forms and patterns in which the tradition of the other voice presented itself have now been sketched. It remains to highlight the major issues around which this tradition crystallizes. In brief, there are four problems to which our authors return again and again, in plays and catalogs, in verse and letters, in treatises and dialogues, in every language: the problem of chastity, the problem of power, the problem of speech, and the problem of knowledge. Of these the greatest, preconditioning the others, is the problem of chastity.

THE PROBLEM OF CHASTITY. In traditional European culture, as in the cultures of antiquity and others around the globe, chastity was perceived as woman's quintessential virtue—in contrast to courage, or generosity, or leadership, or rationality, seen as virtues characteristic of men. Opponents of women charged them with insatiable lust. Women themselves and their defenders—without disputing the validity of the standard—responded that women were capable of chastity.

The requirement of chastity kept women at home, silenced them, isolated them, left them in ignorance. It was the source of all other impediments. Why was it so important to the society of men, of whom chastity was not required, and who more often than not considered it their right to violate the chastity of any woman they encountered?

Female chastity ensured the continuity of the male-headed household. If a man's wife was not chaste, he could not be sure of the legitimacy of his offspring. If children who were not his acquired his property, it was not his household, but some other man's, that had endured. If his daughter was not chaste, she could not be transferred to another man's household as his wife, and he was dishonored.

The whole system of the integrity of the household and the transmission of property was bound up in female chastity. Such a requirement pertained only to property-owning classes, of course. Poor women could not expect to maintain their chastity, least of all if they were in contact with high-status men to whom all women but those of their own household were prey.

In Catholic Europe, the requirement of chastity was buttressed by moral and religious imperatives. Original sin was inextricably linked with the sexual act. Virginity was seen as heroic virtue, far more impressive than, say, the avoidance of idleness or greed. Monasticism, the cultural institution that dominated medieval Europe for centuries, was grounded in the renunciation of the flesh. The Catholic reform of the eleventh century imposed a similar standard on all the clergy and a heightened awareness of sexual requirements on all the laity. Although men were asked to be chaste, female unchastity was much worse: it led to the devil, as Eve had led mankind to sin.

To such requirements, women and their defenders protested their innocence. Following the example of holy women who had escaped the requirements of family and sought the religious life, some women began to conceive of female communities as alternatives both to family and to the cloister. Christine de Pizan's city of ladies was such a community. Moderata Fonte and Mary Astell envisioned others. The luxurious salons of the French *précieuses* of the seventeenth century, or the comfortable English drawing rooms of the next, may have been born of the same impulse. Here women not only might escape, if briefly, the subordinate position that life in the family entailed but might make claims to power, exercise their capacity for speech, and display their knowledge.

THE PROBLEM OF POWER. Women were excluded from power: the whole cultural tradition insisted on it. Only men were citizens, only men bore arms, only men could be chiefs or lords or kings. There were exceptions that did not disprove the rule, when wives or widows or mothers took the place of men, awaiting their return or the maturation of a male heir. A woman who attempted to rule in her own right was perceived as an anomaly, a monster, at once a deformed woman and an inadequate male, sexually confused and consequently unsafe.

The association of such images with women who held or sought power explains some otherwise odd features of early modern culture. Queen Elizabeth I of England, one of the few women to hold full regal authority in European history, played with such male/female images—positive ones, of course—in representing herself to her subjects. She was a prince, and manly, even though she was female. She was also (she claimed) virginal, a condition absolutely essential if she was to avoid the attacks of her opponents. Catherine de' Medici, who ruled France as widow and as regent for her sons, also adopted such imagery in defining her position. She chose as one symbol the figure of Artemisia, an androgynous ancient warrior-heroine who combined a female persona with masculine powers.

Power in a woman, without such sexual imagery, seems to have been indigestible by the culture. A rare note was struck by the Englishman Sir Thomas Elyot in his *Defence of Good Women* (1540), justifying both women's participation in civic life and their prowess in arms. The old tune was sung by the Scots reformer John Knox in his *First Blast of the Trumpet against the Monstrous Regiment of Women* (1558); for him rule by women, defects in nature, was a hideous contradiction in terms.

The confused sexuality of the imagery of female potency was not reserved for rulers. Any woman who excelled was likely to be called an Amazon, recalling the self-mutilated warrior women of antiquity who repudiated all men, gave up their sons, and raised only their daughters. She was often said to have "exceeded her sex" or to have possessed "masculine virtue," since the very fact of conspicuous excellence conferred masculinity even on the female subject. The catalogs of notable women often showed those female heroes dressed in armor and armed to the teeth, like men. Amazonian heroines romp through the epics of the age—Ariosto's *Orlando Furioso* (1532), Spenser's *Faerie Queene* (1590–1609). Excellence in a woman was perceived as a claim for power, and power was reserved for the masculine realm. A woman who possessed either was masculinized and lost title to her own female identity.

THE PROBLEM OF SPEECH. Just as power had a sexual dimension when it was claimed by women, so did speech. A good woman spoke little. Excessive speech was an indication of unchastity. By speech, women seduced men. Eve had lured Adam into sin by her speech. Accused witches were commonly accused of having spoken abusively, or irrationally, or simply too much. As enlightened a figure as Francesco Barbaro insisted on silence in a woman, which he linked to her perfect unanimity with her husband's will and her unblemished virtue (her chastity). Another Italian humanist, Leonardo Bruni, in advising a noblewoman on her studies, barred her not from speech, but from public speaking. That was reserved for men.

Related to the problem of speech was that of costume, another, if silent, form of self-expression. Assigned the task of pleasing men as their primary occupation, elite women often tended toward elaborate costume, hairdressing, and the use of cosmetics. Clergy and secular moralists alike condemned these practices. The appropriate function of costume and adornment was to announce the status of a woman's husband or father. Any further indulgence in adornment was akin to unchastity.

THE PROBLEM OF KNOWLEDGE. When the Italian noblewoman Isotta Nogarola had begun to attain a reputation as a humanist, she was accused of incest—a telling instance of the association of learning in women with un-chastity. That chilling association inclined any woman who was educated to deny that she was, or to make exaggerated claims of heroic chastity.

If educated women were pursued with suspicions of sexual misconduct, women seeking an education faced an even more daunting obstacle: the assumption that women were by nature incapable of learning, that reasoning was a particularly masculine ability. Just as they proclaimed their chastity, women and their defenders insisted on their capacity for learning. The major work by a male writer on female education—*The Education of a Christian Woman: A Sixteenth-Century Manual*, by Juan Luis Vives—granted female capacity for intellection but argued still that a woman's whole education was to be shaped around the requirement of chastity and a future within the household. Female writers of the following generations—Marie de Gournay in France, Anna Maria van Schurman in Holland, Mary Astell in England—began to envision other possibilities.

The pioneers of female education were the Italian women humanists who managed to attain a literacy in Latin and a knowledge of classical and Christian literature equivalent to that of prominent men. Their works implicitly and explicitly raise questions about women's social roles, defining problems that beset women attempting to break out of the cultural limits that had bound them. Like Christine de Pizan, who achieved an advanced education through her father's tutoring and her own devices, their bold questioning makes clear the importance of training. Only when women were educated to the same standard as male leaders would they be able to raise that other voice and insist on their dignity as human beings morally, intellectually, and legally equal to men.

THE OTHER VOICE. The other voice, a voice of protest, was mostly female, but also male. It spoke in the vernaculars and in Latin, in treatises and dialogues, plays and poetry, letters and diaries and pamphlets. It battered at the wall of prejudice that encircled women and raised a banner announcing its claims. The female was equal (or even superior) to the male in essential nature—moral, spiritual, intellectual. Women were capable of higher education, of holding positions of power and influence in the public realm, and of speaking and writing persuasively. The last bastion of masculine supremacy, centered on the notions of a woman's primary domestic responsibility and the requirement of female chastity, had not as yet been assaulted—although visions of productive female communities as alternatives to the family indicated an awareness of the problem.

During the period 1300–1700, the other voice remained only a voice, and one dimly heard. It did not result—yet—in an alteration of social patterns. Indeed, to this day they have not been completely altered. Yet the call for justice issued as long as six centuries ago by those writing in the tradition of the other voice must be recognized as the source and origin of the mature feminist tradition and of the realignment of social institutions accomplished in the modern age.

We thank the volume editors in this series, who responded with many suggestions to an earlier draft of this introduction, making it a collaborative enterprise. Many of their recommendations and criticisms have resulted in revisions, though we remain responsible for the final product.

PROJECTED TITLES IN THE SERIES

Giuseppa Eleonora Barbapiccola and Diamante Medaglia Faini, *The Education of Women,* edited and translated by Paula Findlen and Rebecca Messbarger

Marie Dentière, *Prefaces, Epistles, and History of the Deliverance of Geneva by the Protestants,* edited and translated by Mary B. McKinley

Isabella d'Este, *Selected Letters,* edited and translated by Deanna Shemek

Cassandra Fedele, *Letters and Orations,* edited and translated by Diana Robin

Maria de Gournay, *The Equality of Men and Women and Other Writings,* edited and translated by Richard Hillman and Colette Quesnel

Annibale Guasco, *Discussion with D. Lavinia, His Daughter, concerning the Manner of Conducting Oneself at Court,* edited and translated by Peggy Osborn

Olympia Morata, *Complete Writings,* edited and translated by Holt N. Parker

Isotta Nogarola, *Selected Writings,* edited by Margaret L. King and Albert Rabil Jr. and translated by Diana Robin, with an introduction by Margaret L. King.

Christine de Pizan, *Debate over the "Romance of the Rose,"* edited and translated by Tom Conley

François Poulain de la Barre, *The Equality of the Sexes* and *The Education of Women,* edited and translated by Albert Rabil Jr.

Olivia Sabuco, *The New Philosophy: True Medicine,* edited and translated by Gianna Pomata

Maria de San Jose, *Book of Recreations,* edited and translated by Alison Weber and Amanda Powell

Madeleine de Scudéry, *Orations and Rhetorical Dialogues,* edited and translated by Lillian Doherty and Jane Donawerth

Sara Copio Sullam, *Apologia and Other Writings,* edited and translated by Laura Stortoni

Arcangela Tarabotti, *Paternal Tyranny,* edited and translated by Letizia Panizza

Lucrezia Tornabuoni, *Sacred Narratives,* edited and translated by Jane Tylus

A SMALL WORLD:
THE VENETIAN CONVENT
OF CORPUS DOMINI

THE OTHER VOICE

An age-old and enduring tradition sees convents as dumping grounds for girls who were ugly, sickly, or otherwise unsuited for marriage. This tradition was very much alive in fifteenth-century Italy, among clergy and laity alike. "The man who has a misshapen or mutilated daughter gives her to Christ," the Florentine layman Franco Sacchetti commented sardonically; and he was echoed from the pulpit by the great Franciscan preacher Bernardino of Siena, who chastised his audience for this practice: "I have heard that if you have [a daughter] who is blind or lame or crippled, you at once place her in God's service: you put her in a convent."[1] But it was not just physical deformities that led to forced enclosure of young women: economic pressures too could lead parents to place their daughters in convents. No respectable marriage could be contracted without a dowry, and dowries rose sharply and steadily throughout the late Middle Ages, leading patrician men like Dante Alighieri to long for the good old days when the birth of a daughter didn't stir fear in her father.[2] A family cursed with too many daughters faced hardship or even ruin, and the financial interests of the lineage sometimes dictated that one or more of the girls enter a nunnery as brides of Christ (who, oddly, com-

1. Iris Origo, *The World of San Bernardino* (New York: Harcourt, Brace and World, 1962), 64 and 270. This line of interpretation has its modern exponents, such as the historical demographer David Herlihy, "Some Psychological and Social Roots of Violence in the Tuscan Cities," in *Violence and Civil Disorder in Italian Cities, 1200–1500,* ed. Lauro Martines (Berkeley: University of California Press, 1972), 146: "Girls who lacked a sufficiently large dowry or physical beauty, and who had slight hope of finding a husband, were placed in the convents with equal haste."

2. Dante Alighieri, *Paradiso,* 15.103–5. On dowries and the marriage market in Renaissance Italy, see Julius Kirshner and Anthony Molho, "The Dowry Fund and the Marriage Market in Early Quattrocento Florence," *Journal of Modern History* 50 (1978): 403–38; Anthony Molho, *Marriage Alliance in Late Medieval Florence* (Cambridge: Harvard University Press, 1994); and Trevor Dean and K. J. P. Lowe, eds., *Marriage in Renaissance Italy* (Cambridge: Cambridge University Press, 1997).

manded a far smaller dowry than a mortal husband). Fathers saved money and
kept the family patrimony intact; convents were filled and the regular round of
prayer and worship was guaranteed; and the excess female population was
ensured a decent livelihood and decorous life—albeit one that these poor
women had not chosen, and generally would not have chosen, for themselves.
Bernardino was alert to the resentment harbored by reluctant nuns and be-
moaned its consequences for the religious life: "When they are grown-up,
they curse their fathers and mothers, saying: 'They have put me here so that I
should have no children, but I will have some, to spite them!'"[3] By the seventeenth century, the imagined rebelliousness of these vocationless nuns had
matured into the fierce diatribes of the Venetian Arcangela Tarabotti (1604–
52), which laid bare the confluence of social, economic, political, and religious interests that sustained the institution of female monasticism and bit-
terly denounced the paternal tyranny that had condemned her and thousands
like her to a monastic hell.[4]

Sister Bartolomea Riccoboni came from the same city and social class as
Arcangela Tarabotti, but her chronicle and necrology of the Venetian convent
of Corpus Domini tell an entirely different story, a story of female dedication
and self-determination. According to Sister Bartolomea, Corpus Domini was
an exemplary convent, filled with women who definitely wanted to be there
and cited by papal bulls as a model for similar religious institutions as far away
as Pisa and Rome. The nuns had chosen the religious life for themselves, often
over the opposition of their families. Some had entered the convent as girls,
others as young women facing an unwanted marriage or as widows; but all
were deeply committed to their collective enterprise, a community of work
and worship. Members of this female community gathered their energies and
organized their lives while each found scope for her particular talents and in-
clinations. And the community gave them a privileged vantage point from
which to observe and comment on events in the outside world, the tempests
that shook the Catholic Church and the most serene republic of Venice—not
to mention their own cloistered world.

The chronicle and necrology of Corpus Domini constitute a precious
source for the history of female piety, a history that for too long has been writ-

---

3. Origo, *World of San Bernardino*, 64.

4. I am echoing the titles of two of Tarabotti's works: *Tirannia paterna* and *Inferno monacale*. The former was published under the pseudonym Galerana Baratotti and with the title altered into the less
polemical *La semplicità ingannata* (Leiden, 1654); an English translation by Letizia Panizza is in
preparation for this series. The latter was edited by Francesca Medioli as *L'"Inferno monacale" di Arcangela Tarabotti* (Turin: Rosenberg e Sellier, 1990). On the problems of forced cloistering and convent discipline, see Romano Canosa, *Il velo e il cappuccio: Monacazioni forzate e sessualità nei conventi
femminili in Italia tra Quattrocento e Settecento* (Rome, 1991).

ten from sources either crafted by male authors or recorded and transmitted by male scribes. Inevitably such sources offer a cloudy lens on the past, one that reveals "not so much what women did as what men admired or abhorred. . . . It is therefore especially important for future historians to turn to detailed study of those works in which women wrote about their own visions and mystical experiences and about life among the sisters in their households, beguinages, and convents."[5] The convent chronicle and necrology of Corpus Domini speak directly to this need: they are early unmediated examples of women's writing, and they describe the lives and deaths of unexceptional women engaged in a common religious enterprise. Moreover, these texts present the lives of this cloistered religious community and its inhabitants at a particularly dramatic moment in the long history of the Catholic Church, when the Great Schism divided western Europe between two competing popes. Far from being closed in upon themselves and interested exclusively in their own spiritual lives, the sisters of Corpus Domini were deeply engaged in the world beyond their walls. And that outside world was equally interested in (and involved in) the affairs of Corpus Domini: friends and relatives came to visit the sisters in the convent's parlor, where they could exchange information and opinions, and to attend mass in the convent's church, where they could hear the sisters take their stand on the issues that divided the church. The religious literature of the late Middle Ages is rich in texts in which male clerics record and comment on the words and deeds of female mystics and holy women. But Sister Bartolomea's ample biography of Giovanni Dominici (the convent's founder and spiritual director) and the many pages of the chronicle devoted to Gregory XII and the events of the schism represent a rarity for that time and place: a female writer commenting on public events and their male protagonists. And it is worth noting that Sister Bartolomea's occasional laments about her limited abilities and inadequacy to the task of writing are purely formulaic expressions of humility. The evidence of the text itself shows her to be fully capable of treating, with clarity of perception and vigor of expression, the events of both the small world of Corpus Domini and the larger world of which it was so thoroughly a part.

CORPUS DOMINI OF VENICE

Corpus Domini was built by the combined efforts of an elderly abbess, a wealthy donor, two orphaned girls and their guardians, and a Dominican

---

5. Caroline Walker Bynum, "Religious Women in the Later Middle Ages," in *Christian Spirituality*, vol. 2, *High Middle Ages and Reformation*, ed. Jill Raitt with Bernard McGinn and John Meyendorff (New York: Crossroad, 1987), 121–39; the quotation comes from 136.

preacher.[6] The abbess, Lucia Tiepolo, had grown up in the Benedictine convent of Santa Maria degli Angeli on the island of Murano, which she entered when she was only eleven. After more than three decades in that convent, she was named abbess of the convent of Sant'Apostolo, one of several Benedictine monasteries and convents on the island of Ammiano in the Venetian lagoon. This was an unattractive post, for these isolated convents had been hit particularly hard by the population decline that followed the Black Death of 1348 and were slowly being abandoned; and Tiepolo accepted it with the greatest reluctance. After three miserable years spent imploring divine guidance and seeking a way out, her prayers were finally answered with a vision of Jesus as the Man of Sorrows, bound to a column all bloody and crowned with thorns, who commanded her to go to Venice and found a convent in his name. She leaped at the task, though it took six years for her to secure the necessary permissions, locate and acquire a suitable site, and set about constructing a small church dedicated to Corpus Domini, the Body of the Lord.

Lucia Tiepolo built the church of Corpus Domini on a spit of land at the extreme northwest edge of the city, a spot so out of the way that few Venetians even knew of its existence. Fortunately, one of those who did was a pious patrician named Francesco Rabia, who generously supported Tiepolo and her church. He financed the construction of a stone church to replace the original wooden structure, provided for its maintenance, and helped Tiepolo build a dormitory to house her nascent community. The seven cells of the wooden dormitory seemed more than adequate for a group that consisted of just the abbess, one other nun, and two lay sisters, and Francesco Rabia remained good-naturedly skeptical of Tiepolo's prediction that someday her convent would house more than sixty women. For over twenty-five years this prophecy showed no signs of coming true; but Tiepolo persevered in her resolve, much to the puzzlement of those who could not fathom why she would want to live in such a deserted place.

The transformation of Corpus Domini from a struggling Benedictine nunnery into a thriving Dominican convent came about at the initiative of two resolute young orphans and their guardians. The girls, Isabetta and Andreola Tommasini, longed to dedicate themselves to the religious life. Their guardian, Margarita Paruta, sought the advice of her confessor, Giovanni Do-

6. The fundamental sources for the early history of Corpus Domini are the texts presented here. The most thorough study of the convent is a *tesi di laurea* prepared at the Università degli Studi di Padova under the direction of Prof. Antonio Rigon: Maria Ricci, "Il monastero del Corpus Christi di Venezia fra Tre-Quattrocento (con una silloge di trentadue documenti inediti)," academic year 1982–83.

minici (1355–1419), a fiery Dominican preacher and one of the most influential religious figures in Venice.[7] At first Giovanni suggested the girls enter the Augustinian convent of Sant'Andrea. But then he, Isabetta and Andreola Tommasini, and another devout woman received a series of visions directing them to build a convent where the church of Corpus Domini stood. Giovanni obtained the consent of Lucia Tiepolo, who agreed to resign her title as abbess of a Benedictine nunnery and become prioress of the new Dominican community. He traveled to the papal court to win the pope's approval and used his connections among the Venetian patriciate to secure political and financial support for the project.[8] The most important contribution, however, came from the Tommasini girls themselves, who used their dowries to construct the convent, and from Margarita Paruta's husband, Marco.

During the year it took to build the convent, the community that was to inhabit it took shape. Giovanni Dominici vested a handful of women (including Lucia Tiepolo and Isabetta and Andreola Tommasini) with the Dominican habit in preparation for the day when their new home would be ready, and he persuaded a score of others to join them. In effect, they formed a large and well-organized community even before they entered the convent. The new convent of Corpus Domini was consecrated on June 29, 1394, in a ceremony in which members of Doge Antonio Venier's family participated, and on that day twenty-seven women—a mix of adolescent girls, young unmarried women, and widows—took their vows.

From this substantial base, Corpus Domini rapidly grew to become one of the largest and most eminent houses in Venice: as Sister Bartolomea noted proudly, "in nine days we numbered forty; by the end of the year we were fifty; and within two years there were seventy-two of us." Most of these women sprang from the Venetian patriciate. Thanks to their family connections and the convent's good reputation, their influence reached far beyond the convent walls. Within a few years of its founding, the convent of Corpus Domini had created a lay confraternity of the same name, which bore the consecrated Eucharist through the city in annual processions; by the middle of the fifteenth century these processions had evolved into one of the major festivals of the

7. For biographical information on Giovanni Dominici, see Stefano Orlandi, *Necrologio di S. Maria Novella* (Florence: Olschki, 1955), 2:77–126; Giorgio Cracco, "Giovanni di Domenico Banchini," in *Dizionario biografico degli italiani*, vol. 5 (Rome, 1963), 657–64. On his influence in Venice, see Daniel Bornstein, "Giovanni Dominici, the Bianchi, and Venice: Symbolic Action and Interpretive Grids," *Journal of Medieval and Renaissance Studies* 23 (1993): 143–71.

8. Giovanni described his journey to the papal court in a letter known as the "Iter perusinum," published in Giovanni Dominici, *Lettere spirituali*, ed. Maria-Teresa Casella and Giovanni Pozzi, Spicilegium Friburgense 13 (Freiburg: Edizioni Universitarie, 1969), 186–93.

MAP 1. Jacopo de' Barberi, perspective view of Venice (1500) (Museo Civico Correr). The doge's palace and Piazza San Marco are in the middle of the picture, immediately above Neptune's head. The Dominican church of San Zanipolo can be seen on the far side of Venice, above and to the right of San Marco. Corpus Domini is on the point of land at the upper left of the plan.

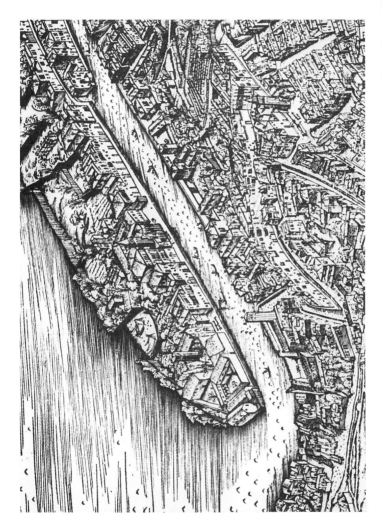

MAP 2. Detail of Jacopo de' Barberi, perspective view of Venice, 1500 (Museo Civico Corer). Detail of map 1 showing the convent of Corpus Domini. The convent complex occupies the tip of land known as Capo de Zirada. The church of Corpus Dimini faces the Grand Canal; to its left, surrounding the cloister, are the dormitory, parlor, sheds, and other buildings of the convent complex. The parish church of Santa Lucia with its bell tower can be seen a few buildings to the right of Corpus Domini.

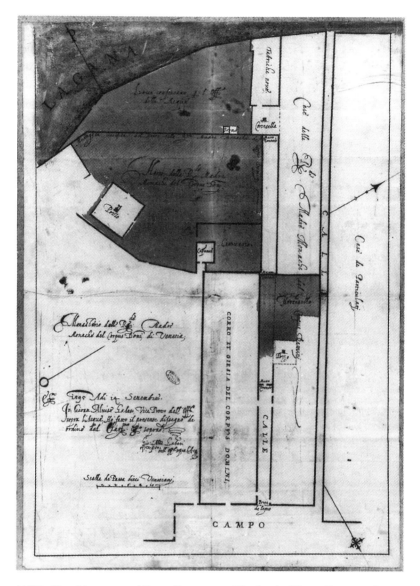

MAP 3. Plan of the convent of Corpus Domini, 1595. The church of Corpus Domini, in the center of the plan, is flanked to the right by the lodgings of the nuns. Behind the church are shown the bell tower, cemetery, vegetable garden, well, oven, and sheds for washing and drying the laundry. Beyond them lie the waters of the Venetian lagoon. The other buildings of the complex are not shown, their place being occupied by the plan's legend. Venice. Ground plan of the Monastery of Corpus Domini, anno 1595. Corporazioni religiose soppresse, Corpus Domini, b. 1, N. 1. Photoreproductions were prepared by the Sezione fotoriproduzione of the Archivio di Stato in Venice. By permission of the Ministero per i Beni e le Attività Culturali (permission no. 41, dated 25 August 1999)

liturgical year, sponsored by the Venetian government and involving all the major confraternities.[9] Corpus Domini attracted donations and bequests not only from women who joined the community and their kin, but also from wealthy patricians and prominent churchmen who were impressed by the piety of the sisters and sought the benefit of their prayers. Between 1440 and 1444, with the financial backing of Fantin Dandolo (a Venetian nobleman who became bishop of Padua in 1448) and of Tommaso Tommasini (bishop of Feltre—and brother of Isabetta and Andreola), the sisters completely rebuilt the church of Corpus Domini.[10] In those same years, and thanks again to the intervention of Bishop Tommaso Tommasini, Corpus Domini also assumed control of the nearby parish church of Santa Lucia, beginning an involvement of these cloistered women in the care of souls that would last for better than thirty years. When their control of Santa Lucia was challenged by another community of female religious, the sisters of Corpus Domini defended their patronage rights over the church and their possession of the precious relics it contained—going so far as to steal the sacred body of Saint Lucy and conceal it under their stairs, thereby provoking the wrath of the patriarch of Venice (who excommunicated them) and the civic authorities (who dispatched masons to brick up all entrances to the convent).

This storm soon blew over, but the concern for property rights did not. By the end of the fifteenth century, records of rents and revenues dominated the convent's archives, as the sisters acquired ever greater wealth and an increasingly sophisticated mastery of accounting methods and administrative techniques.[11] At the same time, the fervor that accompanied the convent's founding gradually gave way to daily routine and conventional devotions. But the religious commitment and spiritual ideals that had inspired Corpus Domini at its inception survived—survived even the legal suppression of the con-

9. Edward Muir, *Civic Ritual in Renaissance Venice* (Princeton: Princeton University Press, 1981), 223–30.

10. Fantin Dandolo (1379–1459) was named archbishop of Candia in 1444 and bishop of Padua in 1448; he was buried at Corpus Domini: Giuseppe Gullino, "Fantin Dandolo," in *Dizionario biografico degli italiani,* vol. 32 (Rome, 1986), 460–64. In addition to being the addressee of Giovanni Dominici's "Iter perusinum," Tommaso Tommasini was bishop, in succession, of several cities in the Venetian sphere of influence: Cittanova, in Istria (1409–20); Pola (1420–23); Urbino (1423–24); Trau, in Dalmatia (1424–35); Recanati and Macerata (1435–40); and Belluno and Feltre (1440–47): Giovanni degli Agostini, *Notizie istorico-critiche intorno la vita e le opere degli scrittori viniziani,* vol. 1 (Venice: Simone Occhi, 1752; reprinted Bologna: Forni, 1975), 450–86.

11. The surviving documents consist of thirty bundles (*buste*) of manuscripts on paper and six bundles of parchments, in the Archivio di Stato, Venice [henceforth ASV]. By 1718 those documents had been organized systematically and provided with an alphabetical inventory, which gives at least a vague indication of what has since been lost: ASV, Corpus Domini, busta 1: Catastico di tutte le scritture del monastero per alfabetto.

vent in 1810 and its physical destruction soon thereafter—in the chronicle
and necrology kept by Sister Bartolomea Riccoboni.

THE CHRONICLE OF CORPUS DOMINI

We know almost nothing about Sister Bartolomea. She tells us that she was a
twenty-five-year-old virgin when she entered Corpus Domini on the day the
convent was founded. But that is all she has to say about herself, her back-
ground, or her role in the convent. She says nothing about her family, perhaps
because, unlike those of so many of her sisters in religion, it did not figure
among the Venetian nobility. She does not even mention that those sisters in
religion soon included her biological sister, Chiara Riccoboni, who had joined
the convent of Corpus Domini by July 1397.[12] She keeps her gaze turned resolutely away from herself and toward the sisters among whom she lived and
the collective life of their community.

She recorded the life of that community in her native Venetian dialect,
the language spoken by the sisters of Corpus Domini, though her prose is also
sprinkled with words and phrases from the Latin liturgy they sang and recited.
She told their story under two guises, in paired literary forms: a chronicle and
a necrology. The necrology provides brief biographies of nearly fifty women
who died in the convent between 1395 and 1436. The chronicle, in contrast,
recounts the history of their collective enterprise, starting with the foundation of Corpus Domini in the late fourteenth century. It offers a vivid picture
of life in this cloistered community, a small world bounded physically by the
convent wall and organized temporally by the rhythms of work and worship.

The first half of the chronicle deals with the foundation of the convent, its
growth, and the communal life of the nuns. Corpus Domini was a convent of
strict cloister, closed off from the outside world by a protective wall and sealed
by a triple-locked gate, with the keys held by three different women. The
world within this wall was arranged into functional spaces: the church where
the sisters worshiped and the cells where they slept; the refectory where they
ate and the chapter room where they assembled to deliberate and to confess
their faults to the community; the infirmary where they cared for the sick and
dying; the sheds where they washed their habits and hung them to dry; the
parlor where they spoke with visitors and heard about the events of the day.
Time, too, was ordered, with the year governed by the liturgical seasons of
penance and celebration and the day structured around the collective prayers
of the community. The monastic office was a demanding round of daily wor-

---

12. Dominici, *Lettere spirituali*, 347.

ship, requiring the sisters to get up in the middle of the night to recite the night office, matins, rise again before dawn for lauds, and then assemble for worship at prime, terce, sext, none, vespers, and compline (at sunrise, midmorning, noon, midafternoon, sundown, and before bed). Such a schedule might seem burdensome, and it is no surprise to find that every so often one of the sisters might doze off after lauds; but in general they found singing the office as sweet as candy and saw devils waiting to pounce on any syllable they let drop out of their prayers.

Because of the strict cloister, the sisters of Corpus Domini shared certain concerns that do not figure quite so prominently in the lives of individual holy women. More than their personal spiritual perfection, they sought to foster the convent community. No one wanted to seem any better than the rest, so they performed their penances in secret and, when enjoined to obtain permission to pursue them, renounced them rather than ask permission. They dedicated themselves to observing the monastic vows of poverty, chastity, and obedience. Nothing they had was their own; everything was the property of the community, and even their clothing was shared. The young women so prized their virginity that they could be suspected of spiritual pride, but even the ancient prioress, Sister Lucia Tiepolo, so feared for her virginity that she hid whenever a doctor visited the convent. Above all, they honored the virtue of obedience, that renunciation of self and will that made it possible for them to live peaceably together year after year. This emphasis on the values of unity and community gives poignant urgency to their efforts to maintain harmony during the later years of the Great Western Schism (1378–1415).

The Catholic Church had been divided for as long as Sister Bartolomea could remember. Ever since a disputed papal election in 1378, the ecclesiastical hierarchy had been split between two competing popes, one based in Rome and the other in Avignon.[13] Europe promptly divided along political lines: France and its allies Scotland, Navarre, Castile, and Aragon supported the Avignon papacy, while England, Flanders, Portugal, Hungary, Bohemia, and most of Germany accepted the Roman pope. Neither side could impose its candidate on the other, neither candidate would step down, and all attempts to negotiate a solution failed. For nearly three decades, the schism dragged on with no end in sight.

New hopes were stirred when the pious Angelo Correr of Venice was elected pope of the Roman obedience in 1406, taking the name Gregory XII.

---

13. Walter Ullmann, *The Origins of the Great Schism: A Study in Fourteenth-Century Ecclesiastical History,* 2d ed. (Hamden, Conn.: Archon Books, 1972); Francis Oakley, *The Western Church in the Later Middle Ages* (Ithaca: Cornell University Press, 1979).

Before the election he (like all the cardinals) promised to meet with his rival, the Avignon pope Benedict XIII, to negotiate an end to the schism. When he failed to fulfill this promise, seven of Gregory's cardinals abandoned him and, together with most of Benedict's cardinals, assembled in Pisa. There political and religious leaders tried to put into practice the conciliar theory—that is, the idea that supreme authority within the church resided in a general council.[14] In 1409 the Council of Pisa attempted to exercise that authority by deposing both Gregory and Benedict and electing a new pope, Alexander V.[15] Although much of Europe, including Venice, recognized Alexander as pope, both Gregory and Benedict refused to resign. The result was rapidly shifting ecclesiastical-political alignments that divided the great international religious orders, such as the Dominicans, and brought pressure to bear on local religious institutions like the convent of Corpus Domini, which were asked to declare their support for the pope recognized by the local political authorities. But Pisa did point the way to a workable solution, and in 1417 the Council of Constance finally succeeded in putting an end to the schism by removing all three contending popes—Roman, Pisan, and Avignonese—and electing Martin V.

In the second half of her chronicle, Sister Bartolomea follows the career of Pope Gregory XII from his election in 1406 to his resignation in 1415 and death two years later, showing us what the women of Corpus Domini knew of papal politics and how they viewed events such as the schism and the Council of Constance. Her account is highly partisan, for Gregory was intimately and inseparably linked with Corpus Domini's founder and spiritual guide. He had been a close friend of Giovanni Dominici ever since their days in Venice, and he associated Giovanni with him in the leadership of the church. Gregory named Giovanni archbishop of Ragusa in 1407 and cardinal of San Sisto in 1408, and he entrusted Giovanni with delicate diplomatic missions to the Holy Roman Emperor Sigismund of Hungary and to the Council of Constance. Sister Bartolomea describes Gregory and Giovanni as a new Moses and Aaron, leading the church through the desert of sin and schism to the promised land of unity and reform. She follows Giovanni in viewing Gregory as a saint, a man blessed with every virtue and free of even venial sin: patient, humble, abstemious, self-sacrificing, pure. She harbored not the slightest doubt that Gregory was the true pope and a true follower of Christ.

Not everyone in Corpus Domini agreed with her. One of the most fasci-

14. Brian Tierney, *Foundations of the Conciliar Theory* (Cambridge: Cambridge University Press, 1955).

15. Aldo Landi, *Il papa deposto (Pisa 1409): L'idea conciliare nel grande scisma* (Turin: Claudiana, 1985).

nating and dramatic passages of the chronicle describes how the rift in the ecclesiastical hierarchy was replicated within the small world of the cloister.
This chapter forms a bridge between the first and second halves of the chronicle, linking the life of this community of women with the schism that divided
the church at large—or more precisely, that split the ecclesiastical hierarchy.
In its early stages, the schism seems to have concerned mostly prelates and
theologians, though as it persisted some troubled people began to see this institutional crisis in apocalyptic terms and turn nervously to the obscure
promises and threats of prophets, seers, and visionaries.[16] But as soon as we
move outside the small circle of those who had a pressing professional interest
in ecclesiology (or an idiosyncratic personal one), concern about the rift in the
church falls off sharply. Only when the governing authorities, for essentially
political reasons, suddenly dumped one pope and declared for another—that
is, after the Council of Pisa met with widespread but not universal success—
did people worry seriously about which pope was legitimate: the one they had
acknowledged yesterday or the one they were supposed to acknowledge
today.

That is precisely what happened in Venice in 1409, when the Venetian
government and Venetian church accepted the legitimacy of the pope elected
by the Council of Pisa.[17] It was at this point that the schism that divided the
church at large split the Venetian convent of Corpus Domini. Two-thirds of
the sisters followed Giovanni Dominici's lead in recognizing the Roman pope,
Gregory XII; one-third accepted the choice of their city and of the master general of the Dominican order, Leonardo Dati of Florence, and recognized the
Pisan pope. Their private differences of conscience became public in the
liturgy, which contained a veritable touchstone, a proof text for papal allegiance: a prayer for the pope's well-being.[18] The sisters sought to paper over
their differences and preserve unity by simply praying for "the pope"; but this
did not satisfy the watchful authorities, who ordered them to pray for the pope
by name—and menaced them with excommunication and exile if they named

16. Roberto Rusconi, *L'attesa della fine: Crisi della società, profezia ed apocalisse in Italia al tempo del grande scisma d'Occidente (1378–1417)* (Rome: Istituto Storico Italiano per il Medio Evo, 1979).

17. On Venice's relations with Gregory, see Dieter Girgensohn, *Venezia e il primo veneziano sulla cattedra di S. Pietro: Gregorio XII (Angelo Correr), 1406–1415*, Quaderni 30 (Venice: Centro Tedesco di Studi Veneziani, 1985); Dieter Girgensohn, *Kirche, Politik und adelige Regierung in der Republik Venedig zu Beginn des 15. Jahrhunderts* (Göttingen: Vandenhoek und Ruprecht, 1996).

18. Earlier in the schism, divisions among the clergy of Orvieto similarly became open in the liturgy, when some prayed for Boniface IX of Rome and some for Clement VII of Avignon; peace was restored when each priest was allowed to say his prayers in his own fashion. Luca di Domenico Manenti, *Cronaca*, ed. Luigi Fumi, in *Rerum Italicarum Scriptores*, new ed. (Città di Castello: S. Lapi, 1903), vol. 15, part 5, 401.

the wrong one. To escape this sentence, whenever the task of leading the sisters in prayer fell to one of Gregory's partisans, she "voluntarily" ceded her place to one of the Pisan party. This fended off the threat of exile but brought great hardship to the convent: its supporters were generally in Gregory's camp, and they angrily stalked out of Corpus Domini—and cut off their financial support—when they heard the Pisan pope John XXIII named in the sisters' prayers. Here indeed we have a dramatic (and rare) instance in which the identity of the true pope mattered desperately.

Paradoxically, it was inside this cloistered world that the schism was most inescapably present. For most people the schism was no more than a distant rumbling that could easily be closed out and ignored. Each parish, each town, each bishopric had its pope, whom it recognized as legitimate without caring whether some faraway people recognized some other pope. The sisters of Corpus Domini, in contrast, were locked in with one another, observing their common ideal of strict cloister with other people whom they knew thoroughly and respected just as thoroughly. They could not deny or ignore their religious differences, nor could they demonize those who held opposing views. And because they prized so highly the values of unity and harmony, the schism that divided their community tore at their hearts and souls. For five long years the sisters of Corpus Domini strove to preserve the unity of their community while respecting individual convictions. In the end they succeeded in this delicate task, allowing Sister Bartolomea to conclude (with a hint of justifiable pride): "Our consciences remained unblemished and untroubled by any vexing pricks, because both of the parties acted with good intentions."

THE NECROLOGY OF CORPUS DOMINI

In the very first year after the convent was enclosed, death took one of the sisters: a thirteen-year-old novice named Paola Zorzi. On that occasion, and at each subsequent death, Sister Bartolomea recorded the event and added a few words about the person who had just passed to her heavenly reward. Necrologies like that of Corpus Domini had their distant origins in lists of the names of people to be commemorated day by day throughout the year on the anniversaries of their deaths.[19] But they evolved into something closer to the obituary

19. For an example of such a traditional necrology, see Annamaria Facchiano, *Monasteri femminili e nobiltà a Napoli tra medioevo ed età moderna: Il necrologio di S. Patrizia (secc. XII–XVI)*, Fonti per la Storia del Mezzogiorno Medievale 11 (Altavilla Silentina [Salerno]: Edizioni Studi Storici Meridionali, 1992).

notices found in modern newspapers: brief descriptions of the life and achievements of the deceased.[20] Like the authors of modern obituaries, Sister Bartolomea sometimes resorts to standard phrases and clichéd expressions of appropriate sentiments. But what is most striking about her brief biographies is how highly individualized they are. She describes the characters and long-ings of her sisters in religion, their cultural formation and intellectual accom-plishments, their devotional attitudes and their fortitude in illness. She traces the life events and spiritual paths that led both adolescent girls and elderly widows to the convent, pinpointing the personal meaning their faith held for these women. Since the necrology also includes a lengthy biography of Gio-vanni Dominici, the convent's spiritual father and a key adviser to Gregory XII, it (like the chronicle) confirms the nuns' informed interest in the "male" business of ecclesiastical politics while keeping the life and concerns of this fe-male community very much to the fore.

The women of Corpus Domini came from a variety of social backgrounds and display a range of spiritual preferences. The community included lay sis-ters, young novices, and professed nuns, virgins and widows—and several of these widows were startlingly young, hardly more than children themselves. Some had come to Corpus Domini after years spent in other convents, either Benedictine or Augustinian; and these women, accustomed as they were to collective worship, showed a particular fondness for choral prayer. Even when she needed a cane to get about, the aged Sister Maruzza Contarini hobbled off as fast as she could every time the bell summoned her to choir. But the cheer-ful performance of chores and service to others could also be a form of wor-ship. In particular, those who entered as widows carried into the convent their habits of household management and busied themselves looking after the complex and tending the other sisters. Sister Piera of Città di Castello "tended all the sick women and washed all their filth, and she did not abandon them un-til she saw that they were either dead or out of danger." Like Jesus of Nazareth or Saint Francis of Assisi, she embraced her leprous companion and kissed her sores, and died blessedly as a result of her charity.

Such heroic self-sacrifice gets singled out for praise. So too does the learning of sisters like Diamante, who "always studied the Holy Scriptures and had an excellent intellect for reading and singing and writing," and Isa-betta Tommasini, who seemed like a theologian when she preached in chap-ter. Sister Bartolomea shares none of the misgivings about learning that so

---

20. One well-known example comes from the friary to which Giovanni Dominici belonged in Florence: Orlandi, *Necrologio di S. Maria Novella*.

troubled her spiritual father, Giovanni Dominici.[21] For all his formidable erudition, this lecturer in theology looked upon books and learning with profound suspicion, viewing them as perilous temptations that could deflect people from the high road to God. Sister Bartolomea, in contrast, mentions the medical skills of Lucia Tiepolo almost in passing, as a useful source of income when she was trying to gather the funds needed to build Corpus Domini, and celebrates the wisdom of Isabetta Tommasini, whose advice was sought by men and women alike, without the slightest hint that this might be a source of spiritual pride.

Visions could hardly be claimed as a special gift, since so many of the sisters of Corpus Domini received them. Visions confirmed the presence of the Christ in the consecrated Eucharist. They disclosed the devils that swarmed about the sisters and tried to trip them up and the angels that attended and assisted them. They reminded the sisters of the long lines of saints—especially virgin saints and Dominican saints—who had preceded them on the thorny path they had chosen for themselves, and they strengthened their resolve to persevere. They reassured the bereft community that a departed sister had received her heavenly reward, as when Sister Diamante appeared clad in glorious garments or Maruzza Contarini was seen in the celestial convent reserved for those who love God perfectly. And they proclaimed that their convent was divinely ordained, that it was God's will that Lucia Tiepolo leave her former convent and found this new one dedicated to the body of Christ. In this instance, of course, God's expressed will conveniently matched Tiepolo's own wishes, and one might wonder how often the sisters of Corpus Domini were bending God to their will rather than conforming themselves to his.

Worldly pride was another obvious temptation, for many of the sisters came from aristocratic backgrounds. Their family names read like a roll call of Venice's ruling elite, resonant with wealth and glory: Paruta, Dandolo, Tiepolo, Contarini, Rosso, Pisani, Valaresso, Marin, Zorzi, Corner, Da Canal, Moro, Venier—patrician surnames of doges, admirals, and senators as well as of Bartolomea Riccoboni's sisters in religion.[22] Sister Bartolomea makes little

21. Giovanni may be best known today for his attack on humanistic education, the *Lucula Noctis*, ed. Edmund Hunt (Notre Dame: University of Notre Dame Press, 1940). Coluccio Salutati's reply to Giovanni's polemic is found in his *Epistolario*, ed. Francesco Novati, Fonti per la Storia d'Italia 15–18 (Rome: Istituto Storico Italiano, 1891–1911), vol. 4, part 1, 205–40. For further discussion of Giovanni's attitude toward learning, see Daniel Bornstein, "Dominican Friar, Lay Saint: The Case of Marcolino of Forlì," *Church History* 66 (1997): 259–61.

22. For an identification of the leading families within the Venetian patriciate, see Stanley Chojnacki, "In Search of the Venetian Patriciate: Families and Factions in the Fourteenth Century," in *Renaissance Venice*, ed. J. R. Hale (London: Faber and Faber, 1973), 47–90.

of their social status, perhaps because to any Venetian reader it would have been too obvious to mention. She certainly was not indifferent to such concerns, since she notes that several of the women who came to Corpus Domini from distant cities sprang from noble lineages. Geronima dei Cancellieri was the daughter of the count of Pistoia and the widow of a knight. Onesta dei Marchesi was "from a great lineage, very elegant and notoriously worldly," and her brothers were "all great lords who held castles"; she brought with her to Corpus Domini a little entourage, Piera and Tommasa of Città di Castello, who accompanied her in life and in death. These aristocratic foreigners heard of Corpus Domini from Giovanni Dominici, who recruited them for his convent while on preaching campaigns in Tuscany. They answered his call despite the objections of their families, which sought to dissuade them with mockery or detain them by force. In Sister Bartolomea's necrology, they figure as object lessons in renunciation of the world: though born to social eminence and material comfort, they fled such vanities and chose instead to serve God and their sisters in religion with charity and humility. In the world outside the convent walls, they would have been Sister Bartolomea's social betters; but here they cooked her meals and nursed her when she fell sick.

Despite their careful elimination of markers of status, the sisters of Corpus Domini were not blind to the distinction brought by learning or lineage, or by office. Sister Bartolomea distinguishes between the professed sisters who had made their monastic vows, the novices who had not yet professed, and the lay sisters who did not have the right to sit in chapter. She records the deaths of only three lay sisters, and she does so with notable brevity; Sister Maria Palazzi's thirty-six years in the convent earned her only the barest and blandest of death notices, while Sister Ambrosina is remembered mainly as a quiet and hardworking servant who did the dirtiest chores with never a complaint. The choir sisters shared in such chores and won the community's praise for doing so; but their principal duty was worship. Reciting the monastic hours required a certain level of literacy, which was sufficiently common in the convent that the task of leading the sisters in prayer (the office of hebdomadary) could rotate weekly. Other offices involved more elaborate duties and presumably were held for longer terms: the novice mistress reared the young novices and trained them in the monastic life; the sacristan looked after the church and its furnishings; the wardrobe mistresses cleaned the sisters' habits and distributed clothing as needed. The chief offices, on the other hand—that of the prioress who headed the convent and the vicaress who assisted her—were held for life, or until the holder proved physically unable to perform her duties. These tended to be occupied by women of outstanding learning or wealth or prestige: Lucia Tiepolo, Geronima dei Cancellieri, Isabetta Tommasini, Lucia Dandolo, and Margarita Paruta. It is these women (and the spiritual director of the convent, Giovanni Dominici) who receive the most extensive memorials in Sister Bartolomea's necrology.

THE SPIRITUALITY OF CORPUS DOMINI:
THEMES AND TENSIONS

Sickness and physical pain figure prominently in the necrology, which repeatedly praises patience in illness and fortitude in the face of death.[23] So many of the sisters suffered from debilitating diseases that kept them bedridden for years, and so many of them died while still relatively young, that one suspects there might be some truth to the idea that families tended to dedicate sickly girls to the religious life. On the other hand, this attention to illness might be the natural consequence of the circumstances under which the necrology was composed: since it was the death of each sister that furnished the occasion for her biography, the cause of her death was very fresh in Sister Bartolomea's mind. What distinguished the sisters of Corpus Domini was not so much the dreary facts of disease and death as their attitude toward them. Crippling injuries and catastrophic illness were all too common features of medieval life, afflictions their victims typically bore with loud laments or grim resignation. The sisters of Corpus Domini instead welcomed their sufferings as occasions for spiritual growth, for joyous conformity with the crucified Jesus. Such spiritualization of illness, like illness itself, appears to have marked female piety to an extraordinary extent: an analysis of the life histories of hundreds of medieval saints has shown that illness was "a prominent feature of female holiness, the one category of activity in which women were not merely statistically overrepresented but constituted an absolute majority."[24]

Other characteristic themes of female piety run through both chronicle and necrology: devotion to the Eucharist; intense affective engagement with the person of Jesus, as child and as spouse; a propensity for visions; and ascetic practices aimed at controlling and punishing the body through flagellation and renunciation of food and sleep and at turning the body to spiritual ends

23. The evidence from Corpus Domini can be compared with that from the great English monastery Westminster Abbey: Barbara Harvey, *Living and Dying in England, 1100–1540: The Monastic Experience* (Oxford: Oxford University Press, 1993).

24. Donald Weinstein and Rudolph M. Bell, *Saints and Society: The Two Worlds of Western Christendom, 1000–1700* (Chicago: University of Chicago Press, 1982), 234–35.

through eager identification with Christ's Passion.[25] The sisters of Corpus Domini received Communion far more often than the minimum obligation of once a year, at Easter; indeed, Giovanni Dominici was criticized for giving them Communion too frequently.[26] But they longed to have the body of Christ in them, even as they were in the body of Christ, Corpus Domini. They took in that body with their eyes as well as their mouths, adoring the consecrated Eucharist on display in its tabernacle; and when a sudden gust of wind knocked over the vessel and spilled the consecrated hosts, they were dismayed at this tragic desecration of their Lord's body. They saw Jesus in the host, as a lovely child, and in visions, as a heavenly spouse. They yearned to be with him and to be like him: when Sister Gerolama Mercanti was at the point of death, she "stretched out her arms like a cross, tilted her head to the right side, and rendered her soul to her spouse Jesus Christ, who chose for himself this pure virgin." They fasted and kept vigil and flagellated themselves, conforming themselves to the suffering Jesus. Their spiritual director, concerned that they were harming themselves, ordered them to take food and to turn in their whips and chains; they humbly obeyed, and he was dumbstruck at how many they heaped before him.

In this instance Giovanni delicately balanced encouragement of the sisters' heroic asceticism with reasonable restraint—and such measured sensitivity may seem surprising in someone known as a fierce polemicist, ever ready to stake out extreme positions and defend them resolutely. But profound tensions marked many of these themes in the spirituality of Corpus Domini. The sisters hungered for the Eucharist yet feared contact with an object so awe-

---

25. For surveys of late medieval devotional practices, see Richard Kieckhefer, "Major Currents in Late Medieval Devotion," in *Christian Spirituality*, vol. 2, *High Middle Ages and Reformation*, ed. Jill Raitt with Bernard McGinn and John Meyendorff (New York: Crossroad, 1987), 75–108; R. N. Swanson, *Religion and Devotion in Europe, c. 1215–c. 1515* (Cambridge: Cambridge University Press, 1995); and Daniel E. Bornstein, *The Bianchi of 1399: Popular Devotion in Late Medieval Italy* (Ithaca: Cornell University Press, 1993), 8–42. On female piety in late medieval Italy, see Daniel Bornstein and Roberto Rusconi, eds., *Women and Religion in Medieval and Renaissance Italy* (Chicago: University of Chicago Press, 1996). On the spirituality of Corpus Domini in particular, see Lia Sbriziolo, "Note su Giovanni Dominici, I: La 'spiritualità' del Dominici nelle lettere alle suore veneziane del Corpus Christi," *Rivista di Storia della Chiesa in Italia* 24 (1970): 4–30, and Pawel Dobrowolski, "Piety and Death in Venice: A Reading of the Fifteenth-Century Chronicle and the Necrology of Corpus Domini," *Bullettino dell'Istituto Storico Italiano per il Medio Evo* 92 (1985–86): 295–324.

26. Raymond of Capua also had to defend and justify his practice of giving Catherine of Siena frequent—even daily—Communion: Raymond of Capua, *The Life of Catherine of Siena*, trans. Conleth Kearns (Dublin: Dominican Publications, 1980), 288–91. On eucharistic piety, see Caroline Walker Bynum, "Women Mystics and Eucharistic Devotion in the Thirteenth Century," in her *Fragmentation and Redemption: Essays on Gender and the Human Body in Medieval Europe* (New York: Zone Books, 1991), 119–50; Miri Rubin, *Corpus Christi: The Eucharist in Late Medieval Culture* (Cambridge: Cambridge University Press, 1991).

somely holy. They prized humility and valued the common life yet wondered which ones among them were especially beloved of God. They invoked the emotionally charged language of kinship to describe their relationship with God and with their spiritual director yet displayed a cool aloofness toward their own families.

This tug and fraying of family ties can be felt throughout the chronicle and necrology of Corpus Domini. Entering the convent did not necessarily mean leaving one's family behind. In a number of cases pairs of sisters or a mother and daughter joined the convent together. The younger girls in particular often entered along with a sibling, so that they would not feel totally deprived of family. The convent could also accommodate kin at the other end of life's journey: Corpus Domini provided the final resting place for one ill and elderly Franciscan tertiary, who was taken in to pass her last few weeks with her daughter, granddaughters, and great-niece, all of them members of this Dominican community. But inevitably, feelings for their sisters in religion often supplanted fading (and not necessarily fond) memories of their natal families. And when Giovanni Dominici deliberately set about reorienting the affections of his spiritual daughters to focus on himself as both father and mother, he provoked the anger of the parents he replaced.[27]

It was not merely that his transfiguration of familial bonds into a new spiritual kinship called into question the traditional ordering of the patrician household—though that was surely an issue in a city that made the well-managed household one of the key analogies for the well-ordered state.[28] Venice was governed by a hereditary aristocracy of noble families whose names were inscribed in the Book of Gold. These patricians, and they alone, enjoyed the right to propose legislation, appoint officials, and hold political office. Too successful an advocacy of chastity could threaten the existence of the patrician family. To be sure, a tension between the religious ideal of celibacy and the social imperative of reproduction has marked Christianity from the very start. But this tension assumed particular force and urgency in the late fourteenth century, when recurrent epidemics of bubonic plague threatened entire populations with extinction and imperiled the survival of families as never before. No more cogent example could be found than Giovanni Dominici himself: when this sole surviving child of a widowed mother decided to enter a religious order, he doomed his lineage to extinction.

27. Daniel Bornstein, "Spiritual Kinship and Domestic Devotions," in *Gender and Society in Renaissance Italy*, ed. Judith C. Brown and Robert C. Davis (London: Addison Wesley Longman, 1998), 173–92.

28. Margaret L. King, "Caldiera and the Barbaros on Marriage and the Family: Humanist Reflections of Venetian Realities," *Journal of Medieval and Renaissance Studies* 6 (1976): 19–50.

Venice was far from impervious to the spirit of religious reform. On the contrary, the maritime city was a great center of spiritual fervor in the years around 1400, and the Venetian patriciate participated fully in these movements of religious renewal.[29] If Giovanni posed a threat to the patrician family, it was precisely because so many men and women were responding to his call, leaving their relatives and their children to become friars and nuns. The convent of Corpus Domini housed women from the leading families of Venice and depended on their kin for support. In return, the convent (like other convents throughout Europe) sustained the social fabric by offering a place of refuge for the bereft, sheltering widows and orphans, the elderly and infirm. It also invoked divine blessings on Venice in moments of political crisis, sending to heaven prayers for peace and prosperity. The cloister and the world both sustained and challenged one another, and it would be hard to say which gazed upon the other with more profound ambivalence.

TEXT AND TRANSLATION

Corpus Domini was a small world of its own; but even if the door was triple locked, the wall that separated the nuns from the world and protected them from its threats was a permeable membrane. The sisters eagerly awaited news from the world outside, especially the doings of their beloved father Giovanni Dominici; and their friends and supporters on the outside came to Corpus Domini to hear mass and to seek the spiritual counsel of the prioress, who was revered for her learning and her knowledge of the Scriptures. Texts, too, circulated through the parlor and in the convent: lives of the virgin martyrs, sermons, histories, devotional songs, and letters of spiritual counsel and consolation. And to these texts the women of Corpus Domini responded with texts of their own production: informative letters to Giovanni Dominici, enlightening sermons by Sister Isabetta Tommasini, and the record of their institutional memory, the chronicle and necrology of Bartolomea Riccoboni.

The chronicle is not a daily record of events. Sister Bartolomea says that modesty held her back from writing for nearly twenty years, so that when she finally took up her pen she produced what had to be a retrospective account, with all the compression and lapses that result from the selective operation of memory. But though she frequently invokes memories—her own and those of

---

29. On spiritual currents in Italy around 1400 with special reference to Venice, see Giorgio Cracco, "La spiritualità italiana del Tre-Quattrocento: Linee interpretative," *Studia Patavina* 18 (1971): 74–116.

the women around her—she did not rely on memory alone. Like all institutions, the convent of Corpus Domini kept administrative records; and examination of the surviving records of the convent confirms that Sister Bartolomea consulted them as she drafted her chronicle. In addition, she drew on more literary works, such as the letters of spiritual counsel that Giovanni Dominici addressed to the sisters of Corpus Domini and, in all likelihood, a history of the schism and of the Council of Constance.

Compiling such chronicles and necrologies was a common practice in monastic institutions, both male and female. Beginning in the fifteenth century, a number of Italian convents—especially those associated with the Observant movements—began to keep convent chronicles. The one kept by the Poor Clares of Monteluce, in Perugia, blended the two genres: the first chronicler, Sister Eufrasia, began writing in 1488 but started with a retrospective glance back to the institution of the regular observance in 1448; death notices are included in sequence in the course of the chronicle as sisters passed away.[30] In Venice, Chiara Riccoboni continued her sister's task of chronicling the history of Corpus Domini; and the convent's 1718 inventory lists *Croniche del monistero* and *Libri delle morte*—using the plural for both convent chronicles and books of the dead.[31] Unfortunately, many of these texts—and not merely those that once resided in Corpus Domini—have been lost to the ravages of time, exacerbated by the suppression of convents and dispersal of monastic libraries, and few of the surviving manuscripts have been published.[32] There are a handful of *Nonnenbücher* from fourteenth-century German convents such as Unterlinden, which give Latin *vitae sororum* comparable to the vernacular biographies of the necrology of Corpus Christi. Those "sister-books" have recently been the object of a fine study by Gertrude Jaron Lewis, and a brief excerpt from the *Lives of the Sisters* of Unterlinden has been translated into English.[33] But to the best of my knowledge this translation of the convent chronicle and necrology of Corpus Domini is the first attempt to make some of these

---

30. *Memoriale di Monteluce: Cronaca del monastero delle Clarisse di Perugia dal 1448 al 1838*, ed. Chiara Agusta Laniati, intro. Ugolino Nicolini (Assisi, 1983).

31. ASV, Corpus Domini, busta 1: L'antichità ravivata, and Catastico di tutte le scritture del monastero per alfabetto.

32. In addition to the *Memoriale di Monteluce* and the texts translated here, see the *Ricordanze del monastero di S. Lucia o.s.c. in Foligno (cronache 1424–1786)*, ed. Angela Emmanuela Scandella with an appendix by Giovanni Boccali (Assisi, 1987). Like the chronicle of Monteluce, this starts from a later date than that of Corpus Domini and provides much fuller information for the modern period.

33. Gertrude Jaron Lewis, *By Women, for Women, about Women: The Sister-Books of Fourteenth Century Germany* (Toronto: Pontifical Institute of Mediaeval Studies, 1996), which includes on microfiche the texts of eight of the nine surviving sister-books; Simon Tugwell, ed. and trans., *Early Dominicans: Selected Writings* (New York: Paulist Press, 1982), 417–24.

works by women, for women, and about women available in their entirety to an English-speaking audience.

The chronicle and necrology of Corpus Domini were originally kept in the convent, but the autograph copies disappeared when the convent was demolished in 1810. Fortunately the texts survive in a number of later copies. Basing themselves on two eighteenth-century manuscripts in Venetian libraries—MS lat. IX 89 (3228) in the Biblioteca Marciana and MS Gradenigo 62 in the Biblioteca del Museo Correr—Maria Teresa Casella and Giovanni Pozzi prepared a critical edition of Sister Bartolomea's chronicle and necrology, which they published as appendixes to their edition of the *Lettere spirituali* of Giovanni Dominici.[34] Just two years later, Casella and Pozzi announced (with some chagrin) the discovery of a number of manuscripts that had been unknown to them when they prepared their edition. Of these, by far the most important was MS Correr 484 (C.I.3), in the Biblioteca del Museo Correr. This collection of texts pertaining to Giovanni Dominici and the convent of Corpus Domini was prepared by Giovanni Domenico Armano, O.P., an active (if not particularly talented or original) participant in the learned circles of eighteenth-century Venice. The value of Correr 484 is that it was "fedelmente copiato da' suoi originali"—faithfully copied from its originals—as Armano declares in the prolix title to his manuscript. In fact, Correr 484 contains some details that were missing from the other copies and clarifies a number of passages that they had obviously garbled. As a result, Casella and Pozzi were able to publish a number of corrections and additions to the text, some of them quite significant.[35] My translation is based essentially on the Casella-Pozzi edition, taking into account their subsequent modifications, though I have also consulted MS Correr 484 directly.

I have sought to produce a translation that is faithful to Sister Bartolomea's Venetian Italian and that also reads smoothly and naturally in English. Those two goals are not entirely compatible: Sister Bartolomea's sentences often sprawl to a length not easily tolerated in English, so I have divided and repunctuated them to clarify, but not alter, her meaning. Rather than replicate her pervasive use of the superlative, I have tried to use terms that convey the sense of "very" or "extremely" or "most" that is rendered in Italian by the ending *-issimo*. I have standardized the spelling of names, preferring (for instance) the more familiar Giovanni Dominici to the Venetian dialect form, Zuan

34. Bartolomea Riccoboni, *Cronaca del Corpus Domini* and *Necrologio del Corpus Domini,* in Giovanni Dominici, *Lettere spirituali,* ed. Maria-Teresa Casella and Giovanni Pozzi, Spicilegium Friburgense 13 (Freiburg: Edizioni Universitarie, 1969), 257–94 and 295–330.

35. Maria Teresa Casella and Giovanni Pozzi, "Giunta al Dominici," *Italia Medioevale e Umanistica* 14 (1971): 131–91; the corrections and additions to the text of the chronicle and necrology are on 172–82.

Domenego. And on rare occasions I have added an explanatory word or two, set off by square brackets.

SUGGESTIONS FOR FURTHER READING

On female religious life: Daniel Bornstein and Roberto Rusconi, eds., *Women and Religion in Medieval and Renaissance Italy* (Chicago: University of Chicago Press, 1996); E. Ann Matter and John Coakley, eds., *Creative Women in Medieval and Early Modern Italy: A Religious and Artistic Renaissance* (Philadelphia: University of Pennsylvania Press, 1994); Penelope D. Johnson, *Equal in Monastic Profession: Religious Women in Medieval France* (Chicago: University of Chicago Press, 1991); Jo Ann Kay McNamara, *Sisters in Arms: Catholic Nuns through Two Millennia* (Cambridge: Harvard University Press, 1996); Gertrude Jaron Lewis, *By Women, for Women, about Women: The Sister-Books of Fourteenth Century Germany* (Toronto: Pontifical Institute of Mediaeval Studies, 1996).

On late medieval religion: Francis Oakley, *The Western Church in the Later Middle Ages* (Ithaca: Cornell University Press, 1979); Denys Hay, *The Church in Italy in the Fifteenth Century* (Cambridge: Cambridge University Press, 1977); R. N. Swanson, *Religion and Devotion in Europe, c. 1215–c. 1515* (Cambridge: Cambridge University Press, 1995); *Christian Spirituality*, vol. 2, *High Middle Ages and Reformation*, ed. Jill Raitt with Bernard McGinn and John Meyendorff (New York: Crossroad, 1987); Miri Rubin, *Corpus Christi: The Eucharist in Late Medieval Culture* (Cambridge: Cambridge University Press, 1991); Caroline Walker Bynum, *Fragmentation and Redemption: Essays on Gender and the Human Body in Medieval Religion* (New York: Zone Books, 1991); Caroline Walker Bynum, *Holy Feast and Holy Fast: The Religious Significance of Food to Medieval Women* (Berkeley: University of California Press, 1987); Rudolph M. Bell, *Holy Anorexia* (Chicago: University of Chicago Press, 1985); Richard Kieckhefer, *Unquiet Souls: Fourteenth-Century Saints and Their Religious Milieu* (Chicago: University of Chicago Press, 1984); Donald Weinstein and Rudolph M. Bell, *Saints and Society: The Two Worlds of Western Christendom, 1000–1700* (Chicago: University of Chicago Press, 1982); Daniel Bornstein, *The Bianchi of 1399: Popular Devotion in Late Medieval Italy* (Ithaca: Cornell University Press, 1993), esp. 8–42.

On women and the family: Margaret L. King, *Women of the Renaissance* (Chicago: University of Chicago Press, 1991); David Herlihy and Christiane Klapisch-Zuber, *Tuscans and Their Families: A Study of the Florentine Catasto of 1427* (New Haven: Yale University Press, 1985); Christiane Klapisch-Zuber, *Women, Family, and Ritual in Renaissance Italy* (Chicago: University of Chicago Press, 1985); Christiane Klapisch-Zuber, ed., *A History of Women in the West*, vol. 2, *Silences of the Middle Ages* (Cambridge: Harvard University Press, 1992); Charles de la Roncière, "Tuscan Notables on the Eve of the Renaissance," in *A History of Private Life*, vol. 2, *Revelations of the Medieval World*, ed. Georges Duby (Cambridge: Harvard University Press, 1988), 157–309; Thomas Kuehn, *Law, Family, and Women: Toward a Legal Anthropology of Renaissance Italy* (Chicago: University of Chicago Press, 1991); Judith C. Brown and Robert C. Davis, eds., *Gender and Society in Renaissance Italy* (London: Addison Wesley Longman, 1998).

On the history of Venice: Frederic C. Lane, *Venice: A Maritime Republic* (Baltimore: Johns Hopkins University Press, 1973); J. R. Hale, ed., *Renaissance Venice* (London: Faber and Faber, 1973); Dennis Romano, *Patricians and Popolani: The Social Foundation of the Venetian Renaissance State* (Baltimore: Johns Hopkins University Press, 1987).

THE CHRONICLE OF CORPUS DOMINI

In nomine Domini nostri Iesu Christi et Sanctissime Marie matris eius et beati Dominici patris nostri. Here begins the prologue to a brief chronicle of the most holy convent of Corpus Domini in Venice, of the sisters of the order of Saint Dominic, in the year 1359.

I, Sister Bartolomea Riccoboni, had the greatest desire to write of the wondrous marvels that our most clement Lord God has performed in this most blessed convent, built in reverence for his holy name some twenty years ago. However, I wrestled within myself at the thought of my inadequacy, since such an undertaking would require wise and learned persons. Rather than continue to resist the Holy Spirit, I have decided to write with this goal in mind: in order that those sisters who follow after us may be properly edified, and that they may have reason to praise the Lord for so many good things and be inspired to live well and follow through on this good beginning. I shall strive to do my best to recount the full truth of what I have seen and heard, and if I do not write as I ought to, I beg my readers to pardon me. If the Lord grants me the grace to praise and glorify his holy name, I will tell step by step, first, of the building of the convent; second, of the day when the women entered it and how it was enclosed; third, of the community and fervor of those women; and fourth, of the glorious deaths of many of them.

I

HERE BEGINS THE CHRONICLE, AND WE SHALL FIRST TELL OF THE CONSTRUCTION OF THAT MOST WORTHY CONVENT DEDICATED TO THE MOST PRECIOUS BODY OF THE GLORIOUS LORD JESUS CHRIST. INCIPIT CAPITULO PRIMO.

There was a woman named Sister Lucia Tiepolo, a nun in the convent of Santa Maria degli Angeli of Murano, which maintained a good reputation and observance [of the monastic rule].[1] This woman entered the convent when she was eleven years old, and she remained there for thirty-four years, living in a holy fashion. It so happened that the Lord God brought about the death of the abbess of the convent of Sant'Apostolo of Ammiano, and as a result the lord bishop sought out this woman and asked insistently that she become abbess of that other convent.[2] She did not want to go and so objected strenuously, saying that she had lived in that convent for thirty-four years and could not imagine changing her residence now that she was old. She resisted fiercely, arguing as best she could with many other words and tears; but the lord bishop enjoined her to obey and she, being a dutiful daughter, could not refuse him, though she went with many tears and a bitter heart, and with the intention of sneaking away and going to some unknown place. She remained there for three unhappy years, continually begging God that he might grant her the grace to be his true servant and to do his holy will. Now, one day when this woman was in tearful prayer between sext and none,[3] almost lost and absorbed in spirit, she let her head droop and, behold, she seemed to hear a person come through the church chatting away. She turned and saw the Lord Jesus in the form of a man tied to the column, all wounded and bloody, with the crown of thorns on his head; and he placed his hands heavily on her shoulders and said, "Go to Venice and build me a convent in my name." She said, "What name should it have?" The Lord answered, "The Body of Christ." She asked, "My

---

1. Santa Maria degli Angeli was a convent of Augustinian nuns on the island of Murano, in the Venetian lagoon. This convent was a fertile seedbed of monastic institutions: women from Santa Maria degli Angeli founded the convents of San Giacomo of Murano and San Girolamo of Venice in addition to Corpus Domini. Flaminio Corner, *Notizie storiche delle chiese e monasteri di Venezia e di Torcello* (Padua, 1758; reprinted Bologna: Arnaldo Forni, 1990), 654.

2. Sant'Apostolo was one of several Benedictine monasteries and convents on the isolated island of Ammiano, in the Venetian lagoon. Malaria, frequent flooding, and a decline in vocations forced many of these communities to abandon Ammiano and transfer to Venice in the fourteenth and fifteenth centuries.

3. That is, in the early afternoon, between noon and 3:00.

Lord, how can I do this? I'm a poor little woman; I have no relatives or friends who I might hope would give a penny to help me." The Lord replied, "Have faith that it will be famous throughout the world and I will be its protector." And he showed her the palms of his pierced hands, saying, "Rejoice, for you will see some great and glorious marvels." She came to herself and stood up, thinking she could catch him, and she looked all over the church but saw nothing. The following three nights she saw the same vision, which kept repeating, "Go and do what I tell you, without delay." And as soon as day dawned, she found an excuse to come to Venice to buy what she needed for her convent, and when she arrived in Venice she went to the lord patriarch Francesco Querini, a most holy man, and recounted her vision.[4] He said to her, "Don't be troubled. Since the Lord tells you that this must be, you need have no doubts."

Something that happened gave her an acceptable reason to leave that convent, so she had a departure permit drawn up and came to reside in Venice, where she eagerly sought to make the vision a reality. She pressed her request to our government that she be allowed to construct a convent dedicated to the Body of Christ, until the measure passed in the Great Council and she was granted permission to build it—though it took a full six years after the vision before she managed to win approval. Once permission was granted, she set about looking for a suitable location; she was shown many sites, but none of them satisfied her. When it pleased the Lord God, she was shown this place called Capo de Zirada, which was a shoal where boats were beached, and it so pleased her that she immediately made arrangements to buy it.[5] The land belonged to certain widowed noblewomen who offered to help her erect the building and to come reside with her. Trusting in the Lord Jesus Christ and in these women, she purchased some lumber; but when it came time to pay for it, the women backed out and she was left on her own. She happened to have some money that she had earned by practicing medicine (she treated great crowds of sick people), and with these funds she paid for the land and the lumber and began to have the church constructed out of wood. When the church was built, she had a stone altar made so that mass could be said on the feast of Corpus Christi, which was just a few days off, and she had the church consecrated. As for the aforementioned women, not much time passed before one came down with a tumor on her face and died in agony, another got married and was killed by her husband, another burned herself up, and the fourth fell into great poverty: so it was that all four died in the greatest misery.

4. Francesco Querini was patriarch of Grado from 1367 to his death in 1372.
5. Capo de Zirada was a sparsely inhabited area at the extreme northwest tip of Venice, where the train station is now located.

II

HOW THE LORD JESUS CHRIST INSPIRED
MESSER FRANCESCO RABIA TO VISIT HER CHURCH

Messer Francesco Rabia, who was then a young man, often came to visit this church, for he was very devoted to an image of Our Lady that was in that church, and every feast day he offered on the altar a large candle and so much money that it covered a large share of the expenses.[6] He persevered in this manner for some time until God, by means of a woman who went to Rome, arranged that a privilege with many indulgences be granted to this church, which inspired people to flock to receive this pardon for a long time, and many people's devotion increased—for before then few people even knew that this city had a church dedicated to the Body of Christ.[7] But this pardon soon ended, because it was discovered that it had not been granted by the pope but rather by someone at [the papal] court at the instigation of the aforesaid woman, and so people stopped seeking the pardon. All this happened by divine dispensation in order to demonstrate what would follow, for the glorious Lord God wished to fulfill what he had promised to his devout handmaiden: that she would see a great convent. When Messer Francesco Rabia saw that this prioress was left all alone, he offered to help her, and so he did. She promptly bought lumber and built a wooden dormitory with seven cells and lived there with one companion dressed in the habit of Saint Benedict and two other women in secular clothing, and she lived on the offerings to the church. Many people asked her, "Tell me, good woman, what are you doing here in this desert place?" She replied, "When it pleases my Lord God, he will see to what he has promised me," and she persevered like this for twenty-eight years.

During the great war that Genoa and other cities waged against our illustrious city of Venice, when it looked as if all would be lost from one moment to the next, Messer Francesco Rabia started to pray with great fervor before the image of the Lord Jesus Christ, saying, "My Lord, I beg you: do not let this city perish, and I promise you, my Lord, to have your church walled." As soon as this offer was made, the enemies who were at our port withdrew to Chioggia, and within a year peace was made.[8] Now, when this Messer Francesco went to

---

6. "Messer" was the honorific term of address used for noblemen, doctors of medicine and of law, and priests.

7. An indulgence allowed a penitent who had confessed his or her sin to substitute for the penance due some other act or work of charity, such as a contribution to the building of a church.

8. The War of Chioggia was brought to a close in 1381 by the Treaty of Turin.

measure the church of Corpus Domini, the prioress saw him and rushed to greet him, saying, "You are the man that the Lord has showed me in vision and said to me, 'This is he who shall build my church, and I shall send you a person who will build the convent, and you will live until you see there more than sixty women.'" Messer Francesco replied laughing, "Good mother, you'll see sixty hens." She answered, "I hope by the precious Body of Christ to see that which he has promised me." And so it was: she saw more than seventy women. Thus the wooden church was demolished and a stone one erected.

III

OF CERTAIN BEAUTIFUL VISIONS OF THE PRIORESS

Before she came to live here, this Sister Lucia saw a gold brood hen with all her chicks, and when she tried to embrace or grasp it, it plunged underground and she saw it no more. On another occasion, a spiritual woman saw in a vision her dead mother, who said to her, "Go to Corpus Domini and receive that pardon for my soul." And she seemed to come there, and when she was at the landing she saw a great multitude of white lambs. Coming from a distance to enter the church, when she reached the door she saw a woman dressed in sky blue who took her by the hand and drew her inside, saying, "Come receive this pardon." She asked her, "Tell me, my lady, what are these animals doing here?" The woman replied, "They are souls for whom this pardon is received, and they derive a great benefit from it." Then she added, "Come, let me show you my house" and led her on top of a mountain and showed her a church, saying, "I caused it to snow as much as this church can hold and hence it was named the church of Saint Mary of the Snow; and so it shall be at my son's church." This woman came to the prioress and told her about the vision. Before the year was out, during the month of August, when the prioress had gone to perform her devotions in the church at dawn, she found that it had snowed in one spot enough to cover an altar. The snow was frozen solid; she tried to sweep it away but could not. It lasted for seven days, and everyone who saw it marveled at this miracle. In this manner the Lord showed that he wanted the main altar built there, and so it was done. Shortly thereafter the prioress saw that when the stone to build the church had been purchased and unloaded in that spot, a crowd of children gathered and scampered over these stones and acted as if they were grasping something with their hands, and they leaped about laughing and having a lot of fun. They said that they saw many curly-haired little children and many other fine things that they didn't know how to explain because of their youth; and many other fine things were seen that I will leave out so as not to ramble too much. This holy prioress also said to me, "Believe me, dearest daughter, my Lord will yet make this convent extend as far as Santa Lucia, which will also be ours."[9] Another vision was seen by one of the first women who wanted to enter the convent. She had a great desire to serve God, but her relatives opposed her, saying, "Why do you want to go perish from hunger in a new convent that still has nothing?" Nonetheless she entrusted herself to the Lord, and while sleeping one night she saw herself at the door of the church of Corpus Domini. She looked and saw a very handsome gentleman dressed all in the most brilliant gold and with his arms open wide. Turning around and around, he looked toward Santa Lucia and said, "Who doubts that everything is mine and all is mine?" She woke up trusting completely in the Lord God, realizing that this blessed convent would never lack his grace.

IV

HOW THE HOLY SPIRIT TOUCHED THE HEART OF THE VERY REVEREND FATHER BROTHER GIOVANNI DOMINICI, AND OTHER THINGS THAT HAPPENED

Since the glorious Lord Jesus Christ wished to fulfill what he had promised to his servant—that she would yet see a great convent—he touched the hearts of two virgin sisters, one of them fifteen years old and the other eleven, the older named Isabetta and the younger Andreola. They were daughters of a very virtuous and upright man and woman; their father was named Messer Facio Tommasini and their mother Lady Zaneta, and she was from the Contarini family.[10] When their father and mother died, these girls were left in the hands of Messer Marco Paruta and his wife, Lady Margarita, who raised them as her daughters and brought them up in the fear of God. Since these girls wanted to serve the Lord God but could not find any place in the city that satisfied them, she revealed their desire to her confessor, Messer Giovanni Dominici of the order of preaching friars, who was then lector and preacher at San Zanipolo

---

9. Corpus Domini took possession of the nearby parish church of Santa Lucia in 1444 and continued to administer it until 1476 when, after a long and bitter dispute, it was handed over to the Servite nuns of the Annunziata. The sisters of Corpus Domini sought to retain possession of the relics of the martyr Saint Lucy, whose uncorrupted body reposed in the church dedicated to her. Even as negotiations with the Annunziata reached a critical point, the sisters of Corpus Domini took the body of Saint Lucy and hid it under their staircase—provoking outraged reactions from both ecclesiastical and civil authorities and generating a mass of documentation that has yet to be thoroughly studied. See Corner, *Notizie storiche*, 251–56.

10. The Contarini were one of the largest and most eminent families in Venice. The Paruta also belonged to the Venetian patriciate.

and a man of great holiness and fame.[11] He advised them to become nuns at Sant'Andrea, since he had no thought of getting involved in creating a convent.[12] But the great God, whose wisdom and will no one can resist, appeared to a sick virgin, his devoted servant, who was an elderly woman of great virtue and reputation. He showed her this Brother Giovanni Dominici and these two sisters with many other women here in this place where the church of Corpus Domini stood and told her that he wanted her to build a convent on that site. Similarly, these sisters also had some beautiful visions on this subject, which I will not write here since they have been recorded elsewhere. When he learned of all these visions, Brother Giovanni Dominici still did not budge, and for a long time he objected that he did not want to get himself embroiled in such things. But the Lord Jesus made his heart race so while he was praying and saying mass that he could resist no longer and determined to go to the [papal] court to request permission to build a convent for women affiliated with the Dominican order. Looking over various sites throughout Venice, he could find to his liking only the one the Lord had prepared. He was told about this woman who lived in the little church of Corpus Domini in the habit of Saint Benedict, and he came to speak with her and told her that if she wished to receive the habit of Saint Dominic, he would build a convent for her and bring many women to join her. She humbly agreed and consented to step down as abbess and become prioress. Once Brother Giovanni had understood her intentions, he set out from Venice and in a few days arrived in Perugia, where the papal court was located at that time, and he presented his request to the holy father on the day of the martyr Saint Agnes.[13] On the octave of her feast he received the bulls in full with everything he had requested. When he returned to Venice, with great rejoicing he set about creating the convent with the aid of the Lord Jesus Christ and of many gentlemen and good *popolari*, and above all Messer Marco Paruta.[14] With the dowries of those two sisters and the grace of the Lord God, it was finished in a year: and the amazing thing was that for the entire year it never rained on workdays, but only at night or on holidays.

11. Giovanni Dominici had been appointed lector at San Zanipolo, the chief Dominican church of Venice, in 1388. He went on to become a leader in the reform of the Dominican order, was named a cardinal by Pope Gregory XII, and figured prominently in ecclesiastical politics during the later years of the Great Schism. His career is recounted at length in the necrology, chapter 31.

12. The Augustinian convent of Sant'Andrea della Zirada was not far from Corpus Domini.

13. Saint Agnes, who was martyred in the early fourth century, is honored on January 21 and 28. Giovanni recounted his trip to the papal court in a letter, known as the "Iter perusinum," addressed to Tommaso Tommasini, Isabetta and Andreola's brother.

14. The characterization of some of these backers as "good *popolari*" indicates that they were well-to-do but not members of the Venetian nobility.

When the convent was completed in its present form, with curtains covering the windows as the sisters wished, he got permission from the holy father and from the master general of the order (who was called Master Raymond) to receive and vest whomever he wished.[15] Even before the convent was completed and enclosed, he vested the aforementioned two sisters and a woman named Sister Margarita Mussolini. He also stripped the habit of Saint Benedict from the abbess and her companion and vested them in the habit of Saint Dominic. They remained like this, with the habit under their other clothes, until they entered the convent together with the other women.

V

OF THE DAY THAT THE CONVENT WAS ENCLOSED, AND OF THE WOMEN WHO ENTERED THAT DAY WITH THE GRACE OF THE HOLY SPIRIT, MAY HE BE FOREVER PRAISED

This blessed convent was enclosed on the feast day of Saints Peter and Paul in the form it has at present, and the women who were to enter were prepared.[16] Brother Giovanni Dominici came with Brother Giovanni Benedetto and Brother Bartolomeo of Pisa and Brother Bartolomeo of Florence and many gentlemen and ladies, and our father Brother Giovanni Dominici said mass outside and consecrated those five women who had worn the habit under their clothing for some time: Sister Isabetta Paruta and her sister [Andreola], Sister Margarita Mussolini, and Sister Lucia Dandolo [and the prioress].[17] When the mass was over, we went inside with the aforesaid friars and with some lay-women, including Lady Margarita Paruta, the doge's daughters-in-law, and the mothers of those being enclosed. We all assembled in chapter and our father preached a devout sermon, and then he and the other friars vested those women who had not yet received the habit. He confirmed the former abbess as prioress and Sister Isabetta Tommasini as subprioress; and since the prioress was extremely old—almost eighty—he named as vicaress Sister Lucia Dan-

---

15. Raymond of Capua, the confessor and biographer of Saint Catherine of Siena, was master general of the Dominican order from shortly after her death in 1380 until his own in 1399.

16. The feast of Saints Peter and Paul is June 29.

17. The presence of two women named Lucia—the prioress Lucia Tiepolo and the vicaress Lucia Dandolo—apparently caused some confusion for the copyist, who left one of them out. The sisters Isabetta and Andreola Tommasini are here referred to by the name of the family that had taken them in after their parents' deaths, perhaps because Margarita Paruta played a prominent role in this ceremony.

dolo, who was forty years old, a widowed woman of fine reputation and very spiritual, who had worn the habit of the Gesuates under the obedience of Sister Agnesina Soler for some time.[18] When the chapter was concluded, we went to the refectory along with the laywomen; Brother Bartolomeo and Brother [Giovanni] Benedetto served the meal.

When we had risen from the table and said none, the laywomen departed.[19] Our father remained behind with the other friars: he stayed with us that whole day and had the chapter summoned and gave us our instructions for living in good observance according to the rule of Saint Augustine and the constitutions of the preaching friars.[20] It would be impossible to express the charity and devotion our father showed for his daughters that day. As he went about designating the cells with their altarpieces, he blessed them all with holy water. Then he said the office of the Virgin together with us in the dormitory and in the choir, to show us how we should perform the devout ceremonies that must be done while saying the office, and left us with his benediction. He went away very pleased. He locked the convent and gave the keys to the prioress and two other women, commanding that these two women together with the prioress should open and close the door when necessary.

Just imagine what joy lingered in those minds that had for so long yearned to be enclosed for love of the Lord Jesus Christ! The women who were enclosed that first day numbered twenty-seven: that is, the prioress, whose name was Sister Lucia Tiepolo; Sister Maruzza Contarini and her companion,[21] the two elderly ladies who constructed the first church; Sister Isabetta Tommasini, Sister Andreola her sister, Sister Margarita Palazzi, Sister Diamante Mussolini, Sister Cecilia Dotto, Sister Margarita Piacentini, Sister Andreola her sister, Sister Maria Rizzi, Sister Caterina Costantini, Sister Caterina Simoni, and Sister Isabetta Verga, who were virgin women between eleven and sixteen years old; Sister Domenica Moro, aged fifty, Sister Maria Tasso, Sister Margarita Rosso, aged twenty-three, and Sister Bartolomea Riccoboni, aged twenty-five, all these virgins as well; Sister Lucia Dandolo, Sister Marina Pisani, Sister Franceschina, mother of the abbot of San Giorgio, Sister Cateruzza Stella, and Sister Cristina dalla Terra, who were widowed women; Sister Marina Valaresso, Sister Caterina dal Pomo d'oro, Sister Maria Palazzi,

18. The Gesuates, or Apostolic Clerics of Saint Jerome, were founded in 1360 by the Blessed Giovanni Colombini, whose cousin Caterina established the female branch of the order. The order was devoted principally to charitable activity.

19. None, the fifth of the canonical hours of worship, corresponds to midafternoon.

20. The rule for Dominican nuns was based on the rule of Saint Augustine, with the addition of constitutions specific to the Dominican order.

21. This unnamed companion is presumably Margarita Mussolini.

and Sister Antonia, another four virgins. All these came as a group that first day.

Another seven were vested a week later: their names were Sister Daria Marin and Sister Orsa da Noale, who were seven years old; Sister Marina Marin and her goddaughter Sister Cita, and Sister Anna Rosso, who were virgins; Sister Orsa da Noale, a widowed woman who was the grandmother of the aforementioned Sister Orsa; and Sister Uliana, a widow. When nine days had passed, seven more women entered. Our father Brother Giovanni Dominici had the pope's permission to vest six women from any convent he wished and make them nuns in this one. When they heard of the good reputation of this convent, they came eagerly: their names were Sister Beruzza Ziroldi, Sister Caterina Rosso, and Sister Orsa Fraganesi, all three of whom were thirty years old; the others were eighteen or younger, and their names were Sister Agnesina Ingegneri, Sister Chiara Marin, Sister Gerolama [Mercanti], and Sister Paola Zorzi.[22] In nine days we numbered forty; by the end of the year we were fifty; and within two years there were seventy-two of us.

Since I have mentioned the day the convent was enclosed, I will note the year in which the first church of the precious Body of Christ was built by the prioress, Sister Lucia Tiepolo, which was 1366. The second construction of the church and of the convent that was enclosed by the hand of our father (who is at present cardinal of Ragusa) took place in 1395.[23]

VI

OF THE COMMUNITY AND UNITY OF THE HOLY WOMEN

It was a true community in true charity: never a vain word, but only talk of the Lord God in all places, since while sleeping, waking and eating, at all hours they called on Jesus. When our father knew that his daughters' minds were filled with the Holy Spirit, he felt the greatest joy. When he saw how they called on Jesus at all hours, he wrote a beautiful hymn that named Jesus a hundred times. Perfect silence was observed, such that from the time compline was said until

---

22. Beruzza Ziroldi's surname is given as Ciriuola in the necrology.

23. Sister Bartolomea's dates are frequently inaccurate: the construction of the first church, for instance, took place in 1375, not 1366 as she says here, and the dedication of the convent was June 28, 1394, not 1395. These errors resulted from the lapse of years between the events and the time when she wrote. Since Giovanni Dominici was named archbishop of Ragusa in 1407 and cardinal of San Sisto in 1408, the chronicle was composed more than a decade after the events described here, if the phrase identifying him as a cardinal is not a later insertion. Sister Bartolomea herself says in the preamble that she had put off writing for twenty years.

mass the following day was finished (that is, the one that is said after the hours) no one would utter a single word.[24] Even the confessors marveled at such perfection, and especially at the great silence. This was because the good father had taught his daughters well; he used to say that he would rather hear that a barrel of wine or oil had been spilled than that a sister had broken the silence. Their fervor reached the point that going to the windows bothered them terribly.[25] Some of the sisters were so given to devotion and meditation that as they walked they seemed to speak with God. Some meditated on the Passion of Christ, saying Our Fathers and doing as many acts of supplication as there were acts in his life. Some others said as many psalters as Christ's person has limbs; still others said two psalters a day; and in this manner all led a holy life. The vicaress had to command them to go easy and temper their great fervor, and she gave them a direct order to take food, since they were so fervent they did not want to eat. When our father saw such perfection and such humility, wanting to sate them with that angelic bread they so craved, he came every Sunday to say mass and give communion to those who wished—which led to his being reproved by some servants of God who did not know how virtuous these women were. He replied that when someone asks him for the holy sacrament and he refuses to give it, may God deprive him of his grace.

These women also practiced great abstinence. Many dragged their mattresses away and slept on bare planks, and they slept very little. They frequented the choir so much that they could hardly wait to go to the office; some of them told me that when they entered the choir they seemed to see an angel that led them in singing God's praises, and they sang the office with such joy that they seemed to be among choirs of angels. Moreover, they tasted such sweetness on their palates when they said the office that their mouths seemed full of every savory candy. When one sister was in ecstasy, she saw white puffs like cotton issue from the mouths of the sisters as they sang the office and fly up to heaven, while the good angel remained very happy by their side; she also saw the devil waiting eagerly to see if anyone left out a syllable, to make a note of it. All day long there were women in ecstasy at all hours, now this one and now that. When the chime sounded they could hardly tear themselves away from prayer to go take bodily food, but obedience constrained them. Some of them ate nothing but bread and the basics.

24. Compline, the last of the canonical hours of worship, followed the evening meal. Once compline had concluded the monastic day, silence was to be observed until the next day began with matins.

25. The windows let in air and light, but also temptations. The sisters of Corpus Domini avoided showing their faces at the windows and engaging in idle gossip with passers-by, limiting their conversations to the barest minimum and offering only words of devout exhortation.

They were well supplied with hair shirts, chains, and whips. Some were so humble that they arranged to go off together in a group to beat themselves, and they scourged themselves with great shedding of blood. As an indication that this humility was pleasing to God, I will recount one miracle that occurred. There were three young women who went every evening to scourge themselves together. One evening they went about this business with such fervor that they were locked out of the dormitory because they had been at it too long. When they sought to come in they found the doors closed and could not open them no matter how hard they pushed. They did not want to knock for fear of being recognized. They stood there quite dismayed, not knowing what they should do. They started to pray, saying, "My Lord Jesus Christ, you know well that we have been moved purely by love of you, and so we beg you, please see that no one knows of this and open the door for us." Having made their prayer, they returned and found the door open. They looked to see whether anybody was around and saw no one, so thanking God they went off quietly to their cells; shortly thereafter came the knock on the cells and matins sounded. God performed many marvels of this sort, so that anyone who wished to recount them all would find the task too long.

When our father observed that many women were falling ill because of their frequent penances and abstinences, he commanded that all the whips and chains be brought to him. When he saw how many there were, he was utterly dumbfounded. He ordered that no one should scourge herself without permission from the vicaress or himself. He did this because he knew they would refrain from asking for this permission, and he likewise ordered them to take food according to their needs, because many rose from table having eaten little.

I shall also speak of the perfect observance [of the rule], and especially of the three principal vows.[26] First of all, as for bodily chastity, may God maintain it as it now is: perfect in the highest degree. The same was true of obedience and poverty of mind and body. When the superiors commanded anything, blessed was she who said yes most promptly. No one would go speak at the windows for any reason without permission, and likewise they maintained with all diligence all the ceremonies of the order. Chapter was held every night, and when they heard that bell they welcomed it as the greatest opportunity, thinking they could humble themselves and announce their defects and accuse themselves of every lapse in conduct. If any little word

26. The three vows of poverty, chastity, and obedience had been the foundation of monastic life ever since the sixth century, when they were enshrined in the rule of Saint Benedict.

passed between them, they immediately admitted their fault before the sun set. They were of such purity and poverty that they did not even hang on to a penny. They had nothing but a quilt and a blanket, a single tunic and a single scapular; when they needed to change, they went to the wardrobe mistress and were satisfied with whatever she gave them. The wardrobe mistresses routinely changed all their tunics and scapulars four times a year; no one recognized her own things. It was lovely to see so many—indeed, all of them—so clean. They did exactly the same thing with the bedclothes: there were two sisters who washed everyone's linens; and those women changed their things, giving them clean and taking away the dirty, and in this way everything was made common. All the alms that were sent to the sisters by their relatives or friends were held in common; many a time those to whom the alms were sent did not know about it. Everything belonged to everyone, and all had their needs met. The Lord God provided for us.

Our father was our procurator and kept us supplied with everything necessary; all the officials went to him as daughters go to a good father, and like a good father he provided everything with great charity.[27] In addition to the living expenses, he bought so much cloth that everyone had what she needed. There was no need to ask our relatives, since he provided for everything. Indeed, I often saw this marvel: more bread was cleared from the table than had been set out. God performed many wonders that I shall omit for brevity's sake, but in them one can recognize how pleased God is with the religious life when unity and charity are joined with observance of the three principal vows. I can truly say that many were so steeped in obedience that if the prelates had said, "Throw yourselves into the fire," they would have done so. Our venerable father Brother Giovanni Dominici procured for us and governed us for five years, and he provided for us in both spiritual and temporal matters. I have already spoken of temporal things. As for the spiritual, he consecrated us and preached every day during Lent and many times during the year; he wrote to us and explained all the books that were needed for the office and for masses during the whole year. Because of his good reputation, our convent loomed larger in the devotion of many people, and especially of many gentlemen who adorned our sacristy with chalices and vestments and everything that was needed—thanks to our father, who provided us with everything, as I said already. In short, we were like a child at its mother's breast, without the slightest care or thought.

The convent remained without its vineyard for six years after it was enclosed (while Sister Lucia Tiepolo was prioress), and what is more, the cells on

---

27. The procurator was legally empowered to act on behalf of the cloistered community.

that side were without windows.[28] But our Lord Jesus Christ, who has always looked after his maidservants, inspired the hearts of certain men and women—including Messer Piero Vicaran and Messer Nicoletto Zane and Lady Marina Valaresso and Lady Beatrice Giustiniani—who bought us some houses that were attached and enclosed the place for us. Other persons with great devotion and charity saw to it that our walls were raised, the cells' windows opened, and the vineyard planted. Then Sister Margarita Paruta, the second vicaress, built the new dormitory and the parlor; Sister Geronima dei Cancellieri, who was the second prioress, had the parlors inside the sacristy refurbished; and Sister Isabetta Tommasini, who was the third prioress, had the chapter room fixed up and decorated with paintings, while Sister Andreola had the Last Supper painted in the refectory.[29] The aforementioned prioress observed that for thirty years this convent had had terrible problems with water, so she had the big well dug at a cost of 300 gold ducats.

VII

HOW THE LARGE CHURCH OF THE PRECIOUS BODY
OF CHRIST WAS BUILT, AND WITH WHOSE HELP

During the time that Sister Margarita Bocco was prioress,[30] when we were living in very straitened circumstances and had urgent need of an infirmary, our most clement Lord Jesus Christ stirred the heart of our venerable father Messer Tommaso Tommasini, bishop of Feltre.[31] Moved by compassion, he bought the houses of the Diedo family, paying 500 ducats from his own pocket and 100 ducats that we had collected from various people. Those houses of the Diedo family cost 500 ducats in all, and this was in 1436. In 1440

---

28. This paragraph, like the following chapter, may have been inserted later, since it represents a leap forward in time. Lucia Tiepolo, the first prioress, died in 1413. She was succeeded by Geronima dei Cancellieri (died 1431), who served for a decade before falling ill and being replaced by Isabetta Tommasini in 1422 or 1423.

29. The word used for the painting of the chapter room is *istoriar,* indicating that these were narrative paintings. The Last Supper was a standard decoration for monastic dining halls.

30. This chapter is certainly a later insertion, since it recounts events after Sister Bartolomea's death in 1440. The author was probably her sister, Chiara Riccoboni, who made a careful record of the expenditures for this building project (ASV, Corpus Domini, busta 19: Spese della nostra giesa fabricata nel 1440) and wrote an account of the new church's consecration that closely resembles this passage (ASV, Corpus Domini, busta 1: L'antichità ravivata).

31. Tommaso Tommasini was bishop, in succession, of several cities in the Venetian sphere of influence: Cittanova, in Istria (1409–20); Pola (1420–23); Urbino (1423–24); Trau, in Dalmatia (1424–35); Recanati and Macerata (1435–40); and Belluno and Feltre (1440–47).

our gracious God inspired the reverend father Messer Fantin Dandolo (who, bearing great love and devotion for the convent and its women, often visited it and gave lavish alms) and moved his soul to remodel the church. With the agreement of the lord bishop of Feltre and the other procurators and of us women, he set about building the church in the middle of Santa Croce out of reverence for the precious body of the Lord Jesus Christ, to increase people's devotion. He spent 300 ducats at the outset, and construction of the church was begun in 1440 (it was completed in 1444) on November 24, the vigil of Saint Catherine [of Alexandria]. His reverence monsignor the patriarch, Messer Lorenzo Giustiniani, came, as did our reverend father Messer Fantin Dandolo and Messer Tommaso Tommasini and other devout persons.[32] The lord patriarch laid the first stone in the foundation and then came to sing the mass of Corpus Christi, because that day was a Thursday,[33] and when he had sung the mass he gave the sisters a perpetual indulgence of forty days for every time they passed before the high altar and said an Our Father and a Hail Mary. He also gave twice forty days of indulgence to laypersons who would visit the church and give an offering for its construction after the prayers. And when the said church was finished, our venerable father Messer Fantin wanted his reverence Messer Lorenzo Giustiniani, patriarch of Venice, to come and consecrate the church; and this was done with great devotion on July 12. Messer Fantin spent 4,000 ducats to have this church built, and his reverence has given many other alms and goods to our convent. Once the church was consecrated, the Lord Jesus Christ granted that he be named archbishop of Candia, which he resisted firmly; but since the holy father insisted by all means, he accepted like an obedient son on September 13, and on February 20 he was consecrated in our church of Corpus Domini by the hands of the most reverend monsignor, the lord patriarch of Venice, and by the bishops of Ferrara and Jesolo as well, with great devotion and solemnity.[34] On the day our church was consecrated, monsignor the patriarch granted in perpetuity to each person who came to visit the church on that day—that is, July 12—a year's indulgence, and the other two bishops gave forty days each. After the church was built the prioress, Sister Margarita Bocco, had the gratings made

32. The saintly Lorenzo Giustiniani became the first patriarch of Venice in 1451, so this passage must have been revised after that date.

33. He honored the convent of Corpus Domini (or Corpus Christi) by singing the mass for the homonymous feast of Corpus Christi, which is celebrated on the first Thursday after Trinity Sunday.

34. Fantin Dandolo (1379–1459) was named archbishop of Candia in 1444 and bishop of Padua in 1448; he was buried at Corpus Domini. Giuseppe Gullino, "Fantin Dandolo," in *Dizionario biografico degli italiani*, vol. 32 (Rome, 1986), 460–64.

around the inside of our church, using money received with the arrival of sisters, and she also made the two altarpieces of Our Lady. And this is how the church of the most worthy and most precious Body of the Lord Jesus Christ was constructed. But to return to what we were saying, I want to recount a tribulation that I do not think should be passed over in silence.

VIII

HOW THE WIND KNOCKED THE HOLY SACRAMENT DOWN FROM THE PLACE WHERE IT IS KEPT BECAUSE THE DOOR WAS LEFT OPEN

Three years after the convent was enclosed, when the feast of the precious Body of Christ was approaching, the magnificent officers of our confraternity organized a procession.[35] Together with many friars of the order, they devoutly set out from San Geremia carrying large candles in their hands and the sacrament in its tabernacle. Having arrived in our church, the precious consecrated host was placed way up high where it would be safe. And in order that the sisters might receive that spiritual consolation, with our reverend father's permission we kept our little inside door open that whole week. The sisters found very great consolation in this. At all hours of the day and night sisters could be found in the church, and many of them kept their eyes constantly fixed there with many tears and prayers. Some were seen rapt in ecstasy, raised off the earth; others cried mercy, mercy while prostrate on the ground; some spoke to the host and thought it answered them; some saw it in the form of a lovely little child, while others saw it crucified. What a pious sight to see those young women all inflamed and filled with fervor for this most holy sacrament! As the feast of Corpus Christi grew closer, they seemed to lick their lips with desire to be able to contemplate their dear spouse.

The octave of the feast arrived (which that year fell on the vigil of the feast of Saint Peter the apostle), marking three years to the day since the convent was enclosed.[36] After vespers had been sung, when the subprioress was saying the prayer, the wind suddenly sprang up with a great gust that struck the little

35. The feast of Corpus Christi, instituted as a universal feast of the Catholic Church in 1317, was celebrated in Venice with elaborate processions staged by the lay confraternities. See Miri Rubin, *Corpus Christi: The Eucharist in Late Medieval Culture* (Cambridge: Cambridge University Press, 1991), 164–85, and Edward Muir, *Civic Ritual in Renaissance Venice* (Princeton: Princeton University Press, 1981), 223–30. The parish church of San Geremia was in the vicinity of Corpus Domini.

36. In 1397 the octave of Corpus Christi fell on June 28, the day before the feast of Saints Peter and Paul.

window of the tabernacle and knocked over the chalice that holds the hosts left over after the sisters have received communion (though the tabernacle containing the host that had been borne in the procession remained steady). Those hosts tumbled down, and some of them landed on the women who were under the altar—on the heads of some and on the shoulders or chests of others, and one young novice had one of those hosts land in her mouth. No one could express the pain and sorrow the sisters felt. Almost all began to cry mercy, beating their breasts with many tears and sighs as if they were seeing the Lord Jesus Christ dead when they saw those most holy hosts on the ground, and no one knew how to pick them up or dared touch them out of reverence. Our chaplain was summoned; he suggested that the sacristan should wrap her hands in a handkerchief and gather those most holy hosts from the ground, and that is what was done. The sacristan put them in the chalice, and then the chalice was placed on the wheel, and the chaplain put them up in the tabernacle.[37] And from that time forth, that door has no longer been kept open during the octave for fear of such a mishap. When our father heard of this and of our anguish, he wrote us a letter of consolation, saying that we should rejoice and thank the Lord Jesus Christ who had deigned to consecrate our church for himself and had wanted to give his spouses communion himself, and that he was very pleased that this had happened inside rather than outside, since he was glad that the Lord wished his handmaidens to follow their Lord and Redeemer on the way of tribulation.[38] He added many other words, prophesying what would happen to him and how we would remain afflicted and troubled, as indeed came true soon thereafter.

IX

HOW OUR FATHER BROTHER GIOVANNI DOMINICI WAS BANISHED

I will tell of the enormous tribulation that the Lord God sent three years after the affair of the sacrament, which was most burdensome and painful for us. At that time there arose a group called the Bianchi who went throughout the world crying mercy, for which reason many religious men and women and people of every sort were moved to follow them, and everyone dressed in white cloth as they did and set about forming processions through all the cities

---

37. The *ruota*, a sort of lazy susan, allowed objects to be passed in and out of the convent without opening the door to the outside world.

38. See Dominici, *Lettere spirituali*, 70–74 (letter 4).

with the crucifix at their heads, crying and singing mercy with great devotion and tears. And many enemies made peace with one another, for which reason those processions were deemed to work great miracles.[39] When our father saw that the whole world—except for Venice—adopted this devotion, moved by very great piety and faith he made arrangements with many citizens and priests to perform this devotion in this city. He borrowed our crucifix and sang the mass at San Geremia and organized the procession with many men and women, both religious and secular, all singing and crying mercy; and in this manner they came to San Zanipolo. When they arrived at the square, they found one of the heads of the Ten all ready with his officers on behalf of the government: he wrenched the crucifix from the hands of Messer Antonio Soranzo, who was in the lead, broke the arms of the crucifix, and scattered the procession with many insults and injuries to both men and women.[40]

The government was very indignant with our father on this account, since he had organized this procession without its permission. They called a meeting at night—almost the way the Lord Jesus Christ was treated, everyone was shouting "Crucifige, crucifige eum"—and he was banished from Venice for five years; the priest Messer Leonardo [Pisani] and Messer Antonio Soranzo were banished for one year, because they too had been very fervent in this devotion.[41] This happened the night between Thursday and Friday; he left Venice immediately that night, and in the morning his mother and all of us daughters heard the news that we had been deprived of such a venerable father. No one could express the anguish and bitterness of his mother and of all us daughters, our tremendous wailing and laments when we saw ourselves deprived of the many consolations and spiritual and temporal benefits that we had received thanks to our father! He truly loved us like a good father. After his departure alms seemed to stop coming our way, and from that point we had to scrounge for bread, which had not been necessary before: indeed, we used to feed many poor with what we had left over. When our venerable father learned of his daughters' suffering and need, he often

39. The devotional movement of the Bianchi spread through northern and central Italy in the summer and early fall of 1399; the main processions had been over for some time before Giovanni Dominici's procession and arrest on November 18 and his exile on November 21. On the Bianchi movement, see Daniel E. Bornstein, *The Bianchi of 1399: Popular Devotion in Late Medieval Italy* (Ithaca: Cornell University Press, 1993). For a detailed analysis of Giovanni Dominici's procession in Venice, which I argue was not as closely linked to the Bianchi movement as Sister Bartolomea claims, see Daniel Bornstein, "Giovanni Dominici, the Bianchi, and Venice: Symbolic Action and Interpretive Grids," *Journal of Medieval and Renaissance Studies* 23 (1993): 143–71.

40. The Council of Ten was responsible for maintaining public order in Venice. Giovanni's procession violated a decree of the Ten banning all such demonstrations without their express approval.

41. Leonardo Pisani and Antonio Soranzo had been dedicated supporters of Giovanni's activites in Venice, as well as organizers of this procession. The cry of "Crucify, crucify him" is from Luke 23:21; Sister Bartolomea quotes it repeatedly.

consoled us, sending us lovely letters comforting us and strengthening our resolve to persevere in our good behavior.[42]

When the term of his exile was finished, he returned to Venice. No one
could express the rejoicing in this city among all those who were devoted to
him and loved him, and especially his mother and all of us, his daughters, some
of whom had waited to be consecrated by him; and he graciously came in here
and with the greatest devotion consecrated all those who had not yet been consecrated. During that brief time that he stayed in Venice we received great consolation from him; he gave us communion and preached to us and gave us many
spiritual remedies with much fervor and charity. The daughters remained under their father's care for five and a half years until he was banished, and then after six years had passed he returned to Venice and stayed for three months
before going back to Florence. As God promised, he bore great fruit, like a man
who was always eager for God's honor and the salvation of his neighbor. Since
his reverence recognized that the holy father wished to restore unity to the
holy church, he went to the [papal] court to urge the holy father to bring about
this peace. Because the holy father knew that he was a man of great virtue and
wisdom, he named him a cardinal; and as such he has labored long and still
labors for unity. We have been deprived of hearing him for fifteen years now;
but even though he is far away physically, his reverence never ceases to provide
his daughters with whatever he can. We have received 215 ducats since his departure from Venice, and he has promised us that if God lets him live so long as
to see the holy church reunited, he will arrange to have the convent endowed
so that we will have no need for family or friends, but only prayer, contemplation, and study. In this way our good father constantly thought that his daughters should and would be able to remain always united with their dear spouse,
the glorious Lord Jesus Christ, to whom I pray that in his kindly charity he may
grant us the grace that this might be *per infinita secula seculorum. Amen.*

X

**OF THE VINEYARD WALL THAT COLLAPSED
AND THE DORMITORY THAT WAS DAMAGED**

Ab incarnatione Domini millesimo quadringentesimo nono, on the day of Saint
Lawrence, martyr,[43] at the hour of vespers, there was a blast of wind through
the entire city so terrible that the very oldest people said they had never seen

---

42. Giovanni Dominici's feelings for the sisters of Corpus Domini seem to have cooled with the
passage of time: of the forty-one letters to them published in his *Lettere spirituali,* twenty-seven
(two-thirds) were written within three years of Giovanni's departure from Venice.

43. August 10, 1409.

its like in all their days. All those who happened to be out in boats were in trouble; more than three hundred people—men, women, and children— were reportedly drowned on the way from Mestre, and many corpses washed up in the canal of San Segondo. Many houses collapsed; a good many tops of bell towers and churches and chimneys of houses crashed to the earth, so that people could not walk through the streets. They said that if this weather had lasted more than an hour, all Venice would have been demolished. The Lord God willed that we too would have our share of this tribulation, since the peak of the bell tower fell and smashed part of the new dormitory, and one of the chimneys fell on the old dormitory and crashed right through to the floor. The whole face of the vineyard wall that is joined to the parlor fell down and damaged the shed used for washing the sisters' clothing, and many of the trees in the garden were blown over, leaving their roots dangling in the air. We were all terrified by this, especially on account of the wall, since any layperson could come inside the convent. We had to stand guard every night for fear of thieves, until our most clement Lord Jesus Christ provided for us through the intercession of some gentlemen who arranged for us to have 200 ducats, some from the most illustrious government of Venice and some from their own pockets, so that the wall was soon rebuilt.

XI

OF THE TRIBULATIONS WE SUFFERED
ON ACCOUNT OF THE SCHISM

In that same year, after Messer Angelo Correr, a man of great sanctity, had been made pope, an enormous schism divided his cardinals, as a result of which they abandoned him and elected another pope named Pope Alexander [V], and Messer Angelo, who took the name Pope Gregory XII, made our father a cardinal.[44] Our father stood by Pope Gregory because he recognized the authenticity and sanctity of the holy father, and he defended him with all his might. This Alexander managed to gain the allegiance of almost the whole world—that is, all the realms and the leaders or rulers of cities—while few

44. Angelo Correr of Venice was elected pope in 1406 and took the name Gregory XII. Before the election he (like all the cardinals) promised to meet with his rival, the Avignon pope Benedict XIII, to negotiate an end to the schism that had divided the church since 1378. When he failed to fulfill this promise, seven of Gregory's cardinals abandoned him and, together with most of Benedict's cardinals, assembled in Pisa. In 1409 the Council of Pisa deposed both popes and elected a new one, Alexander V. Though much of Europe, including Venice, accepted Alexander as pope, both Gregory and Benedict refused to resign, and the schism dragged on for several more years. See Aldo Landi, *Il papa deposto (Pisa 1409): L'idea conciliare nel grande scisma* (Turin: Claudiana, 1985).

stood by Gregory. However, many people and all the servants of the Lord God sided with Gregory, and thus the whole world and all the religious orders, male and female, were divided among themselves. Since we knew our reverend father to be a man of great wisdom and sanctity, and likewise Pope Gregory, we sided with them and remained steadfastly under his obedience.

After a few months had passed, doubt crept into the minds of some of our sisters. Seeing that our most illustrious government of Venice and also our order had given Alexander their allegiance and recognized him as the true pope, they sought the advice of our father confessors, who were divided among themselves and gave counsel that reflected their own convictions. As a result, twenty of our sisters were very troubled in their consciences and said that they wanted to align with the order and accept Alexander as the true pope; those who held that Gregory was the true pope numbered forty-five, which left us deeply divided—and not only us, but the whole world, and especially this noble and magnificent city of Venice. Our most illustrious government saw that the city was divided and reached an agreement with his reverence, monsignor the patriarch, who (thinking this would restore unity) ordered all priests and religious to mention Pope Alexander by name when they said their prayer for the pope. When they heard this command, those of our sisters who supported Alexander wanted to obey. At that time our custom was to say a prayer for the holy father after the *Salve Regina* during the hours of the office, mentioning him by name. But those who supported Gregory did not want to name Alexander, since they felt in their consciences that to do so would be a grave sin. They said, "We do not want to mention anyone by name until peace is restored to the church." This statement was acceptable and pleasing to everyone. But when Alexander's supporters recited the prayer, they boldly invoked Pope Alexander by name in the prayer, saying that they wanted to be in line with our order. When Gregory's backers were hebdomadary,[45] they named no one so as not to betray their consciences, and they felt great discomfort when they heard named someone whom they did not consider to be the true pope, so that we were in terrible anguish. Then it happened that some devout laypeople who would most devoutly come to hear mass and the office in our church, and who were supporters of Pope Gregory and gave us generous alms, got up and left our church when they heard Alexander named and withdrew their alms, so that we suffered great hardship.

Now, those who supported Alexander, seeking to make peace among us, wrote of how we were in schism among ourselves to our most reverend lord fa-

---

45. The hebdomadary was the person appointed to lead the recitation of the canonical hours for the week.

ther the general of the order, named Master Tommaso of Fermo—who was one of the principal figures in bringing about this schism, since he was very insistent that all the brothers and sisters of the order should declare for Pope Alexander.[46] When he heard how we were divided, he instructed his vicar, Master Domeneghin of Venice, to appear in his name and order us under pain of excommunication that we must all name Pope Alexander in our prayer. This vicar came and had all of us sisters assemble in the parlor at the sound of the bell. When we had gathered, he began to praise warmly those of our sisters who sided with Alexander, since they were truly obedient daughters, and he commanded us by obedience and under pain of excommunication that we all must name Pope Alexander in our prayer, and anyone who did not do this would be punished severely as a rebel. We were in great tribulation over this, since those who supported Pope Gregory felt they would be offending the Lord God if they obeyed, because in their consciences they believed that Pope Gregory was the true pastor, while if they disobeyed they would suffer excommunication. This inspired intense prayers with much weeping, and thus we remained in terrible anguish.

In the middle of all this, and before the year was out, this Alexander died, which thoroughly pleased all of Gregory's supporters, since they hoped they would be left in peace. After a few days had passed they elected another pope, who was reputed to have been one of the principal instigators of the schism when they broke with Gregory and went with Alexander.[47] This fellow, so far as I understand, was a malicious man. It was said that he had had Alexander murdered so that he could be made pope and that the cardinals elected him out of fear. For these reasons all the rulers and leaders of cities and lands were displeased at having such a pastor; nonetheless, for various worldly considerations, they gave him their obedience.

Holy week came, when it is the custom to say a prayer for the pope during the mass on Good Friday. All of Gregory's partisans refused to name this third pope, who was called John [XXIII]. Our most illustrious government became very indignant at this, since it seemed that its authority was being flouted, and it issued an order that all friars and priests had to say the prayer for the pope during the mass every day for an entire month, mentioning John by name. For this reason many people—and nearly all the religious—left Venice, since

46. Tommaso Paccaroni of Fermo was master general of the Dominican order 1399–1414.

47. The cardinals of the Pisan obedience elected the archbishop of Bologna, Baldassar Cossa, who took the name John XXIII. This second pope in the Pisan line was later deemed an antipope and so was not included in the official numeration of popes. He acquired such an unsavory reputation that over five hundred years were to pass before Angelo Roncalli took the name John upon his election in 1958, thereby becoming the second (and much more beloved) John XXIII.

they did not want John as pope. Some of those who remained got it in their heads to not say the prayer, for which many were banished from Venice, some for six months and some forever. Never had this city seen such persecution of the servants of God. Then an even stricter injunction was issued: that those male and female religious who would not obey the most illustrious government and name Pope John in their prayers would remain locked in prison for two years and then be banished forever from Venetian territory. This provoked the greatest wails and laments from those who saw themselves constrained to speak against their consciences. It was heartbreaking to see so many servants of God afflicted, not knowing what course to follow: either to speak against their consciences, believing this to be a mortal sin, or to go wandering through the world. No one could express the tribulation that was felt, especially by nuns and women sealed in cloisters. In short, everyone was tormented and afflicted because the holy father did not wish his adversary to be proclaimed to be what he was not.

As I said, all Venice was denuded of the servants of God who left because of this persecution. The women of Sant'Andrea were ready to let themselves be expelled from this city rather than say this prayer.[48] They did not want their chaplain to say it in his church, and were it not for his relatives, the government would have decided to throw them out.

Now, to return to our affairs, our mother the vicaress ordered that the hebdomadary should name Pope John, which his partisans did very willingly; and when it was the turn of one of Gregory's supporters to be hebdomadary, she should ask one of Pope John's to do it for her. This was a great relief for Gregory's partisans, whose confessor secretly sided with Pope Gregory. In the midst of this, our most reverend general died; and his death was a great relief to the entire order, since he was the one who kept the order divided. With his death we could remain in peace, since Master Leonardo [Dati] of Florence was made general and he did not insist that one be named rather than the other.[49] We said the prayer without naming anyone, and thus we could remain united and in good harmony right down to this very day. But we suffered this tribulation of the schism for five years, and in the sixth year we remained in peace by the grace of our Lord God, who tests his servants by letting them travel the road of tribulations. However, through his kind charity our consciences remained unblemished and untroubled by any vexing pricks, because both of the parties acted with good intentions.

---

48. That is, the Augustinian convent of Sant'Andrea, not far from Corpus Domini.

49. Leonardo Dati succeeded Tommaso of Fermo as master general of the Dominican order in 1414 and held that office until his own death in 1425.

XII

OF THE PERSECUTION THAT THE HOLY FATHER SUFFERED BECAUSE OF THE SCHISM, AND OF HOW GOD DELIVERED HIM MIRACULOUSLY FROM MANY PERILS, AND HOW AFTER A HOLY LIFE AND WITH A GOOD REPUTATION HE DIED IN PEACE

Holy Scripture tells us how from the beginning of the world to the present hour the holy church has always been persecuted, and always the Spouse of the holy church has marvelously delivered it from great and powerful tribulations. Whoever cares to go look will find that the holy church—starting with Abel the just, who was the first victim, and continuing to Moses—has often been assailed by the devil's envy by means of wicked men, and it has been sustained and aided by the glorious God by means of just and holy men, from Moses to David and from David to the Lord Jesus Christ, and from Christ to the present time. And this shall continue until the very last day, because this is the church militant and hence anyone who wishes to accede to the church triumphant is called to fight in it—taking the example set by our first knight, the Lord Jesus Christ, and followed by his holy apostles, martyrs, confessors, and virgins and by all his saints and all his elect as well.

XIII

HOW THE HOLY FATHER WAS MADE POPE

Holy Scripture recounts how the people of God were slaves in Egypt for four hundred years under the rule of Pharaoh, who afflicted that people with so many harsh tasks that they did not rest day or night and could never sacrifice to the God of heaven, until the glorious God sent them Moses and Aaron, who freed that people from Pharaoh's hands. Just so we might say that in the present time the glorious God has remembered his Christian people, who, because of the schism, did not know their true pastor and went wandering from the way of truth, since the church of God was divided for thirty years and in the hands of two pastors. One part held that the Roman pope was the true pope, while many others thought it was the one in Avignon; and because of this division those who were true servants of God remained in continuous affliction of spirit, constantly weeping and praying in desire for the unity of the holy church. But our glorious God heeded the groans and heard the voices of his servants and sent another Moses to free the Christian people from the hands of Pharaoh—that is, from the infernal devil who held many under his dominion because of the schism and many other faults. In particular the cardinals, bishops, and priests were corrupted by the sin of simony: they bought and sold the grace of the Holy Spirit for money; they helped themselves to benefices; and thus the house of the celestial Father had become a den of thieves. Every man looked to his own profit, and no one cared about restoring peace and unity in the church of God.

When the Lord Jesus Christ saw how his Father's house was corrupted by sins, he was moved by his usual kindly charity, and in the year 1406 he sent his vicar to right his little boat. This was Messer Angelo Correr, a Venetian nobleman, who was named Pope Gregory XII: a man of great sanctity, a doctor [of theology], adorned with the greatest virtues.[50] When the Roman pope died, by general agreement he was elected as a man zealous for the honor of God and the church, and he humbly accepted with a promise to restore unity, for he had always longed to see the holy church in peace. Since he often demonstrated his feelings for the church, once, while he was still bishop or rather patriarch of Castello, a servant of God told him that he had seen his name written in three colors, black, red, and gold; the black signified that he was a bishop, while the red indicated that he would be a cardinal and the gold that he would be pope. Hearing this, he said in reply, "If the Lord God allows this to come to pass, I shall strive to see that unity is established. I will send to the antipope and, if need be, I will renounce the papacy." He did exactly what he said. Twelve days after his coronation, with his cardinals' approval, he sent a messenger to the antipope in Avignon, saying that he was prepared to renounce the papacy if the antipope would step down as well, in order that the holy church might be led by a single pastor.

This most holy man sent by God, meek and humble like another Moses, struggled to free the Christian people from Pharaoh's clutches, beginning with the clergy. He especially wanted the cardinals to live justly and without simony. He himself, like a true pastor, did not sell benefices for money but lavishly dispensed the grace of the Holy Spirit upon just and worthy persons, and thus he furnished his little boat with good pastors. He created cardinals, bishops, and many prelates who were all men of good life and reputation, and so the holy church began to flourish in the freedom of the Holy Spirit. The glorious God sent him our father Brother Giovanni Dominici as his aid and comfort, almost like another Aaron for Moses, and he always encouraged him in this good initiative and in seeking holy unity. When the holy father wished to do what he had promised—negotiate with the antipope—he could not find

50. Angelo Correr, bishop of Castello (that is, Venice), was elected pope on November 30, 1406.

anyone who was willing to go for fear of death, since in the past many had been
very badly mistreated. Our father Brother Giovanni Dominici, like a man who
loves God's honor and desires to see unity with all his heart, wanted to be the
one who went to the antipope; but Pope Gregory saw that he needed his assistance and did not want to send him. He sent his companion, a lay brother
named Brother Matteo, who left San Zanipolo with our father and was his
most faithful companion in all his labors. This man was a true servant of God;
with great fervor he left his wife as a nun in our convent, while out of humility
he preferred to be a lay brother in the order of Saint Dominic under the obedience of our father, who at that time was in charge of the friary of San
Zanipolo.[51]

XIV

HOW THE POPE NEGOTIATED WITH THE ANTIPOPE, AND HOW THE FLORENTINES, OUT OF ENVY, PLOTTED AGAINST GREGORY, THE GOOD AND TRUE SHEPHERD

When Gregory had been made pope in Rome with all the ceremonies ordained by the holy mother church and was accepted by all as true pope, he
sent the aforementioned Brother Matteo to the antipope with a letter of renunciation, declaring that he was ready to renounce if the other would renounce and one person alone be made pope, and that a place should be found
where they could get together within fifteen months to form this union. This
Brother Matteo went and carried the letters to all the lands he traversed, announcing that Messer Angelo Correr had been made pope in Rome with the
name Gregory XII and was accepted by all as true pope. Only the Florentines
were unhappy, because he was Venetian. Stirred by their own envy, they said,
"If we're going to have a Venetian for pope, you should know that he won't last
a year." They said this in the presence of Brother Matteo, and they did so because they wanted a Florentine, since when Innocent was elected pope they
had spent a lot of money at the [papal] court to have a Florentine chosen; but
the Lord God wouldn't allow this on account of their pride.[52]

When Brother Matteo arrived at Avignon, he delivered his message to the
antipope, Benedict.[53] Upon hearing it, he had Brother Matteo seized and

51. The wife of Brother Matteo is not identified in the necrology.

52. Innocent VII was Gregory's predecessor as pope of the Roman obedience from 1404 to 1406.

53. Benedict XIII was pope of the Avignon obedience from 1394 until his deposition by the
Council of Constance in 1417; he died in 1423.

placed in a tower under the guard of four knights. After fourteen days had passed, Brother Matteo was brought before the antipope, who promised him great benefices and also threatened to take his life; but Brother Matteo, steady and strong, was ready to accept a thousand deaths for the holy church. When the antipope saw Brother Matteo's virtue and his loyalty to the person who had sent him, he learned from this excellent example and sent him back to Gregory, with his cardinals' concurrence, saying that he would be willing to come to the city of Savona, where the two of them could meet to negotiate the union. When Brother Matteo returned with the antipope's letters, Gregory and all those who desired peace were thoroughly pleased.

Gregory sent our reverend father to Venice, to see whether the most illustrious government would provide an armed galley to escort Gregory to Savona when the time came; and this was promised to him. Upon our father's return to Rome, he was named bishop of Ragusa, and four Venetians and two Florentines and the bishop of Città di Castello were made cardinals.[54] All were holy men with good reputations. In that one year the most holy Pope Gregory sowed in the field of holy church some good seed so that it might be fruitful, and he strove to uproot bad practices and plant good ones in the vineyard of the Lord. As I said, he wanted all prelates to live honestly and without tyranny. For instance, there was a certain cardinal who had an income of 20,000 ducats a year, and Gregory told him, "Don't display such pomp, but rather share with poor priests." Some of the leading cardinals had never said mass, and there were those among them who had gone fourteen years without confessing; and our father Brother Giovanni Dominici managed to get them to confess.

After the father of the family had sowed the good seed in his field, night came and the enemy of man sowed weeds on top of it and went away; and when time came for the grain to sprout, up sprang the weeds as well [Matt. 13:24–30], since those who were accustomed to eating the fleshpots of duplicity and falsehood in Egypt did not find manna to their taste [Exod. 16:3]. Wolves could not live among lambs. The holy father proceeded in good faith, while the setters of snares betrayed him in secret. Thus the Florentines plotted with one of the leading cardinals, a man named Baldassar, to have Gregory trapped and killed when he came to Savona to restore unity. He did this out of wickedness and greed, because he feared losing his benefices and honors if unity was restored, and he thought that if Gregory was dead they could make a pope more like them. But by God's will the treasonous letters came into the

54. Giovanni Dominici was named archbishop of Ragusa (Dubrovnik, on the Dalmatian coast) on July 29, 1407.

hands of Gregory, who had set out from Rome to go to Savona, while the antipope had likewise left his place to come to Savona. Learning of this betrayal, both of them halted; and Gregory came to Lucca and sent an emissary to the antipope to arrange for another, safer place. These wicked setters of snares had the messenger detained, so that the time limit that had been set for restoring unity would pass and Gregory would seem to have broken his word. When Gregory saw that the time limit was drawing near and no reply was forthcoming, he sent two ambassadors he trusted so that they might make the accord regarding peace and unity. These men lacked the necessary prudence and returned having sown greater discord than before, since the antipope said that he had no desire to go to his death. When Gregory heard this, he was in agony. Since the promised time limit was getting ever closer, he sent back his most faithful follower Brother Matteo, saying that he should choose whatever city he liked that was most convenient to him. He was ready to suffer a thousand deaths, if only unity might be restored. But by the time Brother Matteo arrived, the antipope had changed his mind and said that he did not want to put himself at risk, for which reason Brother Matteo returned to Gregory utterly disconsolate.

When the cardinals saw that the time limit had passed without unity being restored, they took this as a legitimate reason to turn against Gregory. The demon that entered Judas entered two cardinals who had been cardinals before Gregory became pope; and just as Judas betrayed the Lord Jesus Christ, these men betrayed the pope. They sent letters advancing their false arguments to the cardinals of the antipope and many other prelates and rulers of cities, alleging that Gregory had perjured himself, that the term within which he was obliged to restore unity had passed without peace being made, and many other slanders against the truth. While these two traitors remained at court, they did not go to call on the holy father as is customary, and similarly maligned the other cardinals. Astonishingly, the holy father sent to say that they should offer him their obedience, while they, like rebels, demonstrated their wickedness and refused to obey the holy father—and he benignly waited for them to correct themselves and would not inflict on them the penalty they justly deserved for their disobedient double-dealing. Since these men nonetheless feared that their treason would be discovered and the pope would have them killed, they secretly left his court and joined the antipope's cardinals. With financial backing from the Florentines, they summoned the council in Pisa, saying that these two popes were schismatics and forsworn since they had not restored unity. Many people believed this and so went to that council; and thus, just as the princes and priests turned the people against Christ, so these men stirred them against Gregory, so that many cried, "Cruci-

fige crucifige eum." Alleging their false arguments, they condemned Gregory
as schismatic along with the antipope and had them painted on some paper
that they burned in a mock execution, indicating thereby that there no longer
was a pope and that they intended to elect another one. When Gregory
learned of this, he regretted not having detained those two traitors, and said,
"Since I was made pope, I have done nothing that so gnaws at my conscience
as this: that I didn't bring those two traitors to justice."

When Gregory saw that that council was assembling at Pisa, he came to
Siena for greater security. He was very well received there because of the great
devotion they felt for his holiness, and the holy father remained in Siena almost
like another Moses praying and cursing for the holy church. The Council of Pisa
sat for four months and then, on the feast of Saint John the Baptist, when a year
and six months had passed with Gregory as pope, proclaimed a Pope Alexander.[55] When they heard this, all the rulers of the earth withdrew their obedience
from Gregory and offered it to Alexander. The city of Siena recognized that the
Florentines had betrayed the truth and held that Gregory was the true pope, but
to go along with the rest they gave their obedience to Alexander, so that Gregory thought it best to leave Siena.[56] But even before Siena withdrew its obedience, he was abandoned by most of his cardinals, who went to Pisa.

Seeing himself left all alone, Gregory named our father a cardinal along
with four other Venetians, who were very devout men of holy life.[57] Since the
people of Siena had withdrawn their obedience, Gregory departed from there
and came to Lucca. When Cardinal Baldassar learned that Gregory was leaving Siena, he made a deal with the Florentines, promising them lavish gifts if
they would deliver Gregory into his hands; he did this in order to bring him to
Alexander, who would have him burned as a heretic. The Florentines sent
a large force to detain him, but as it pleased God, Gregory, without being
aware of this plot, had set out half an hour before that army reached the pass.
He arrived at Lucca with eight cardinals and many bishops and prelates of
good life, who together with the ruler of Lucca advised Gregory to summon a

55. The Council of Pisa opened on March 25, 1409, and elected Pietro Filargi as Pope Alexander
V on June 17, 1409. Gregory XII had then been pope for two and a half years, not the one and a
half indicated by Sister Bartolomea.

56. Siena withdrew its obedience from Gregory and recognized Alexander on July 4, 1409.

57. Giovanni Dominici was created cardinal of San Sisto on April 23, 1408; the three (not four)
other persons named cardinal with him were Jacopo del Torso and two nephews of Gregory XII:
Antonio Correr and Gabriele Condulmer (the future Eugenius IV). Note that Sister Bartolomea
has reversed the sequence of events: Gregory named Giovanni Dominici and the others cardinals
before the Council of Pisa. Indeed, it was this act that convinced most of the college of cardinals
that he had no intention of fulfilling his promise to restore unity, provoking them to break with
him and convene the Council of Pisa.

council.[58] He wrote to the antipope and to many princes and lords declaring that he had always supported unity, that he wanted everyone to come together to examine the truth, and that this Council of Pisa could not be held since it is not licit for others to convene a council while the pope is alive.

Those wicked folks who had named Alexander pope never ceased sending ambassadors throughout the world with their specious arguments against Gregory and the antipope, claiming that this Alexander of theirs would restore peace in the church. When they heard these arguments, almost all the lords and rulers of cities gave Alexander their obedience, and few of them went to Gregory's council. While Gregory was disputing in his consistory with some lords, among whom were the antipope's ambassadors, an enormous beam dropped from the roof and fell right behind Gregory's shoulders, so that everyone thought they would die; and when the ambassadors saw that Gregory was not dead and that none of them had been harmed, they attributed this miracle to Gregory's sanctity and revered him as Christ's true vicar. However, as soon as a few days had gone by they acted the way sailors do, who forget all about God once the danger is past. Now, when Gregory noted that no one came to his council and that everyone was going to Pisa, and that the ruler of Lucca could no longer host him for fear of the Florentines, he departed and came to Rimini. The lord of Rimini loved Gregory and was his most faithful son, and he firmly defended the truth.[59] For this reason the Florentines and Bolognese together with Baldassar (who was cardinal of Bologna) made war on Lord Carlo [Malatesta] of Rimini, so that he could no longer host Gregory. To save him from being captured, he sent him to Cividale [in Friuli], where he was received with great charity by the lord of Cividale.

XV

HOW GREGORY PASSED THROUGH CHIOGGIA AND TORCELLO AND CAME TO CIVIDALE, AND HOW THE VENETIANS TREATED HIM

When the holy father was about to leave Rimini, he asked the Venetians to grant him safe passage. He would gladly have come to Venice, but the government, seeing that the whole world was recognizing Alexander as pope, did

58. Lucca, which jealously preserved its independence from Florence, was ruled at this time by Paolo Guinigi.
59. Carlo Malatesta ruled Rimini from 1385 until his death in 1429; he and Giovanni Dominici were Gregory's most faithful supporters.

not want him to come to Venice and so had him pass by way of Chioggia and Torcello. When the holy father arrived at Chioggia, nearly half of Venice went to greet him; and when he saw such a multitude of Venetians, he lit up with joy and gave everyone his blessing and many indulgences. He stayed there for two days and then came to Torcello, and there as well great throngs went to meet him. He greeted everyone kindly, from which all those who loved him received the greatest consolation. Even some of those who had given credence to the slander and defamation heaped upon him were moved to devotion when they saw his entirely gracious and humble bearing. One of the leading gentlemen told me that if the doge had seen him he would have won his firm support, since he bore himself so graciously that everyone who saw him said, "This man is a saint." He remained five days in Torcello before departing for Cividale; and when he passed close by Venice, he gazed compassionately upon it and tearfully said, "Oh Venice, Venice, who does not accept the visitor that God sends you."[60]

When he arrived at Cividale, the leader of that city with all the people received him with great charity. Residing in Cividale, he did everything in his power to bring the lambs back to the true shepherd; but the wolves had so blinded the lambs that they did not perceive the truth, and the lord who ruled the city, for fear of war, began to turn against him. Still, all the religious and the entire populace of the city believed that Gregory was the true pastor.

All the religious orders and all the cities and lands were divided among themselves. In Venice especially, everything was in schism. Such an uproar could be heard in the council that it sounded as if they were hacking each other to pieces, since many gave obedience to Alexander and many to Gregory, and for this reason the council was sharply divided. But above all, Messer Michele Sten, doge of Venice, was set against Gregory, since he had wanted one of his nephews to be named bishop and the holy father would not do it because he was not fit for that office.[61] This doge and a few others carried the day over the majority that wanted Gregory, and so they asked for Barabbas and condemned Christ. They held many rancorous meetings, and at the last, which was held on the eve of Saint Augustine, they withdrew their obedience from Gregory.[62] We might well say that this almost repeated the Passion of the Lord Jesus Christ in many respects, since when he went to Jerusalem the

60. Gregory's words echo those of Jesus (Luke 13:34 and Matt. 23:37): "O Jerusalem, Jerusalem, killing the prophets and stoning those who are sent to you!"

61. Michele Sten was doge of Venice 1400–1413, succeeding Giovanni Dominici's close friend and supporter Antonio Venier (doge 1382–1400).

62. After tumultuous debates, Venice declared for Alexander V on August 26, 1409; the principal feast of Saint Augustine is August 28.

whole city went forth to greet him with great festivity crying "rex Israel," and shortly thereafter they asked for Barabbas and crucified Christ, from whom they had received so many benefits. So it was with this his vicar: when he was created pope, all Venice rejoiced and celebrated, sounding the bell for many days and then forming a most solemn procession to San Marco, and then they sent him seven solemn ambassadors, who went with greater pomp than any embassy had ever displayed before. But these honors were transformed into great sorrows, since he suffered more harm from his Venetians than from the other cities. For many cities, when they learned that the Venetians had withdrawn their obedience from him, did the same, whereas if the Venetians had remained firm the others would have done likewise.[63] But just as Christ was condemned by his kin according to the flesh, so was this his vicar.

The Passion of the Lord Jesus Christ was renewed in many ways in this his servant. The night that Gregory was condemned, a certain religious person was praying, offering tearful prayers for Gregory and for this city which was so torn by strife; that person was carried in spirit to the Great Council and heard all the uproar that was being made and saw in their midst the Lord Jesus Christ dripping blood, crucified anew. Many other signs were seen. Some gentlemen who feared God would not go along, and many like rabid dogs cried, "Crucifige crucifige eum"; and so the opposing party triumphed.

When the government issued an order that no one should call Gregory pope, the anguish and suffering of his friends and relatives was beyond words, and the whole populace wept. When Gregory received the news that the Venetians had decided against him, he said, "Blessed be my Lord Jesus Christ, who wishes that I travel the road of martyrdom." The cardinals, together with all those who loved the truth, were stricken almost dead with anguish when they heard the news, since they had hoped to be liberated by the Venetians. They passed that whole night in bitterness, and in the morning they all went to the holy father, thinking they would find him dead; but the holy father had spent that night in prayer with Jesus on the Mount of Olives and had prayed to the Father that he not have to drink from the chalice of the Passion if this might be, but nonetheless that God's will be done. After he had taken comfort in Jesus Christ, seeing that it was the will of the celestial Father that this come to pass, he descended from the mountain and came to his disciples, who had come there to comfort him. When they saw his face joyous and resplendent like the sun—and he genuinely seemed jubilant—everyone who beheld this

63. On relations between Gregory and Venice, see Dieter Girgensohn, *Venezia e il primo veneziano sulla cattedra di S. Pietro: Gregorio XII (Angelo Correr), 1406–1415,* Centro Tedesco di Studi Veneziani, Quaderni 30 (Venice: Centro Tedesco di Studi Veneziani, 1985).

marvel exclaimed, "Truly, this man is a saint." When they wanted to start to talk about these things, the holy father said, "I deserve much worse for my sins." All God's servants and all those who supported Gregory, and especially our sisters of Corpus Domini, prayed without a break for the holy father and for the cardinal our father and for the unity of the holy church, and many of the sisters had lovely visions, so that day and night they never ceased praying with the greatest tears, moans, and sighs.

Now, since the Lord wished to rescue his servants from the lions' jaws, he sent his angel—that is, the king of Apulia, for he alone did not render obedience to Alexander.[64] He sent six armed galleys to the port of Cividale to carry away the holy father and all his followers. When that evil cardinal of Bologna, whose name was Baldassar Cossa, heard that those galleys had gone to carry the holy father to one of the king's cities, he sent many soldiers to lie in wait to seize the holy father when he boarded the galley. The lord of Cividale, who loved the holy father, warned him about that army, and everybody was thrown into despair, seeing that there was no other way to reach the port where the galleys were. But just as the holy patriarch Jacob divided his household in two parts for fear of his brother who persecuted him, so the holy father, enlightened by the Holy Spirit, divided his household. He and his cardinals dressed as chaplains while the archbishop Messer Paolo [Lolli] donned the pope's robes, and disguised in this fashion they set out from Cividale to board the galleys. Their enemies thus fixed their eyes on Messer Paolo in the papal robes, allowing the pope and his cardinals to escape and board the galley. This happened on [September 7], the vigil of the Nativity of the Virgin. All those on the galley received him with great devotion, seeing his bearing so humble and gracious; and when they saw how exhausted he was from his harried flight, everyone pleaded with him to take a little something to eat. He replied with joyous countenance, "I would be ungrateful if I did not fast on the vigil of my dear Mother who has rescued me from such peril. For I must tell you that while I was racing on my horse, I saw a woman shining bright who went before me, reassuring me that I would reach safety." Hearing this, everyone remained greatly edified by him. Then the galleys set sail and with divine assistance he soon arrived in Gaeta, where he was received with the greatest honor and rejoicing. But Messer Paolo was captured in place of the pope and carried off to prison. When his captors saw that they had been tricked and made into fools, they gave him a good many beatings; but he, having rescued the innocent from their clutches, patiently bore every insult.

---

64. As it happened, Ladislaus of Durazzo, king of Naples, soon proved to be an unreliable supporter.

XVI

HOW POPE GREGORY ARRIVED AT GAETA

When the people of Gaeta beheld his sanctity, all held him in the greatest reverence. Even the king often came to visit him, promising to remain loyal to him and fight for him, since only he and his kingdom together with Lord Carlo of Rimini sided with Gregory, while all the rest were with Alexander. Now, after ten months had passed Alexander died, and in eleven days Baldassar Cossa, a thoroughly wicked man, was elected antipope.[65] With great cunning, he persuaded the king to withdraw his obedience from Gregory, promising him the imperial crown if he would support his entrance into Rome. Because he was more interested in his own prestige than in that of the Lord God, this good king accepted the promises of this Pope John [XXIII] and withdrew his obedience from Gregory and gave it to Pope John, and soon thereafter arranged for Pope John (who had been in Bologna) to enter Rome. When Gregory heard this, he begged the citizens of Gaeta to harbor him until he could find some other refuge, and with great charity they all swore they would risk death for him. No one could recount the sorrow and anguish of all those in the holy father's entourage who saw themselves held captive in the king's power. Only Gregory seemed in good spirits, because of the great confidence he always had in God.

When our father the lord cardinal saw that every worldly hope had failed to restore the holy church to peace, he received Gregory's permission to go to the king of Hungary, because he hoped to persuade him to be the means of establishing unity in the church. Having received permission, our father set out with a single servant and went to Hungary in disguise to avoid being recognized.

The holy father, seeing himself in such danger, sent to ask his dearest son, Lord Carlo of Rimini, to receive him. Despite the opposition of the whole world and the threats of John the antipope, like an obedient son this man was ready to risk his life to defend the truth if only he could help Gregory; and so he welcomed him graciously. Now, Gregory's kinsmen and some Venetian gentlemen hired a boat in Gaeta, telling its owner that he should carry Gregory away quietly, because the people of Gaeta had been ordered by the king not to let Gregory leave. And the rulers of Gaeta would have gladly protected and upheld him and done whatever they could to support him because

---

65. Alexander V died on May 3, 1410; Baldassar Cossa (who was rumored to have poisoned Alexander) was elected Pope John XXIII fourteen days later, on May 17.

they loved him and recognized his sanctity, having received many favors from him and witnessed some fine miracles. One of them occurred one day during a procession, when there was such a tremendous flash of lightning that they all thought they would die, and everybody cried, "Have mercy, holy father." As he knelt humbly on the ground praying and making the sign of the holy cross, the lightning ceased and the weather turned splendid. There was pestilence throughout Apulia at that time, except in Gaeta. A horrendously ugly old woman was seen lurking outside the gates of Gaeta, crying loudly and saying, "I cannot remain in this city as long as Pope Gregory inhabits it." When asked who she was, she replied, "I am Death, who is denied access to this city as long as Gregory resides in it."

Now, the holy father was aware of the citizens' goodwill, but because the king expected to find him at Gaeta he wished to depart for Rimini and could not. As soon as the king arrived at the port, before he could disembark the rulers of Gaeta went to meet the king and said, "Oh holy crown, how could you so scorn God's church that you have sold its pastor for 50,000 ducats? Know that you thereby offend Gaeta. We speak to you on behalf of everyone, since we are prepared to ransom him and face death for him." When the king heard these words, he did not disembark in the city so as not to throw the city into an uproar. After three days he sent four knights to Gregory, renouncing his obedience to him. Among them was a kinsman of that antipope who plotted with the canons of Gaeta to secretly deliver Gregory into the king's hands; but the Lord, who enlightens whoever trusts in him, rescued him marvelously in the following manner. A leading citizen of Gaeta, who had given the holy father the use of a beautiful villa as his lodging, immediately went to the holy father and threw himself on his knees, saying, "Holy father, flee quickly, because the canons are trying to hand you over to the king." He immediately broke open a doorway that led into his house, and the holy father with his cardinals and his things passed through that door and went to the marina and boarded a boat. They soon came to the port where the ship was, and the holy father and his entourage boarded the ship and in a few days arrived in Rimini. Oh lovable Lord God, who delights in testing his friends and delivering whosoever loves the truth! Just half an hour after the holy father had fled, the traitor arrived at the house he had abandoned, looking to seize him and carry him to the king; and finding him gone, he remained defeated.

The holy father stayed in Rimini, yearning for the unification of the holy church and praying fervently for it; and while this was going on, our father returned from Hungary. On this account the emperor convened a council to restore unity, inviting all the prelates and theologians of the world to come to a city named Constance, where it would be decided how to restore peace in the holy church.[66] There it was determined that all three popes should step down and a single pope be created as Christ had commanded. The antipope John was the first to resign, hoping that he would be confirmed in office, and he went to Constance with all his cardinals; Gregory and Benedict did not go themselves but sent their ambassadors with promises to resign if everyone would do so. As his representative, Gregory sent our father, who had exposed himself to many perils when he went to Hungary, since he traveled as a poor man with a single companion so as not to be recognized. Many a time he was in mortal peril, imprisoned, beaten, hungry, begging bread from door to door until he came to the emperor, who received him as a true legate and sent him back to Gregory with gifts and a proper entourage. When he arrived in Rimini, the holy father and everyone else received him with great rejoicing and with tears, seeing that he who was their only hope had returned. As I said, the holy father could find no one else who was willing to go to the council; he alone, like an obedient son and zealot for God's honor, prepared himself to go to his death. Since he was going among his enemies and thought he would be killed, he confessed all his sins and set off for the council in good company. The emperor, who loved him greatly, received him with great honor, and nothing was done without his advice. With everyone thus assembled in a general council, many things were undertaken for the reform of the holy church, which I shall not write of here since they have been recorded in another book written by Messer Tommaso Paruta, bishop of Città Nuova.[67]

XVII

HOW THE HOLY COUNCIL CREATED A POPE OF UNITY

Since the council had decided that all three should resign [the papacy], Gregory, as a man who desired unity more than his own advancement, sent Lord Carlo to the council, granting him full liberty to renounce if the others would renounce. When John saw that things were not going as he had expected, he made arrangements to be received by the duke of Austria, and so he fled one night. When the emperor learned that this duke had given him refuge,

---

66. The Council of Constance (1414–18), summoned on the initiative of the emperor Sigismund of Hungary, finally succeeded in putting an end to the schism.

67. That is, Tommaso Tommasini, brother of Isabetta and Andreola and, from 1409 to 1420, bishop of Cittanova in Istria; like his sisters, he is sometimes given the name of the family that took them in after their parents' deaths. He has been tentatively, but without any solid evidence, identified as the author of an anonymous history of the Council of Constance. On the life and literary works of Tommaso Tommasini Paruta, see Giovanni degli Agostini, *Notizie istorico-critiche intorno la vita e le opere degli scrittori viniziani,* vol. 1 (Venice: Simone Occhi, 1752; reprinted Bologna: Forni, 1975), 450–86.

he sent to him with many threats, declaring that he would kill him if he did not turn the antipope John over to him—for which reason he handed him over promptly. Since it was apparent to all that this John had acted against the council and perjured himself, and in light of the evidence of the many wicked deeds he had always done, for which he would have deserved death, he was stripped of his titles and condemned to prison. The emperor entrusted him to one of John's enemies, who held him under close guard in a castle, as he deserved.[68] This was in the first year that the council was assembled to create the new pope.

When the council saw how Gregory had humbly resigned out of zeal for unity, he was highly praised; and to his great honor he remained as legate to Recanati. That other antipope, Benedict, persisted in his stubbornness, so that to his great shame he was condemned as a rebel against unity while our father remained a cardinal in great honor.[69] The whole council praised his goodness and wisdom and also that of Gregory, and the emperor loved him wholeheartedly. God wondrously aids and delivers those who defend the truth, as was manifestly the case with these two saintly men who had suffered so many disgraces and dangers in order to uphold the truth, while the two antipopes who did not act truthfully were left confounded.

After the council had met in Constance for three years, the new and only pope was created and made at God's will. This was on Saint Martin's day, and so he comes to be called Pope Martin V, may Jesus Christ be praised.[70]

XVIII

HOW POPE GREGORY XII DIED

On October 18, 1418, Pope Gregory XII passed from this life.[71] He died with good disposition and reputation, since he who lives well dies well. He was buried with the greatest honor at Recanati, where he was legate, and many sermons were preached about his sanctity. When he was close to death, among

---

68. John XXIII convened the Council of Constance on November 5, 1414. When it became apparent that the council would insist that he resign as pope, John fled the city on March 21, 1415. He was soon detained and remained in custody until December 1417. The council deposed John on May 29, 1415, and accepted the resignation of Gregory XII on July 4. Benedict XIII was not deposed until July 26, 1417, after his last political supporters had abandoned him.

69. Benedict XIII refused to resign or to recognize his deposition by the Council of Constance, and he continued to consider himself the sole legitimate pope until his death in 1423. Hardly anyone shared his opinion.

70. Ottone Colonna was elected pope on November 11, 1417, and took the name Martin V; he was pope from 1417 to 1431.

71. Sister Bartolomea is off by a year: Gregory died in 1417.

his many notable words he said this: "I have not known the world, and the world has not known me." This can be understood and confirmed by the evidence of his holy conversation and life. He did not know the world in its carnal delights, since he died a pure virgin—and our father, who heard his general confession, bears witness to this. He did not know the world through pomp or pride: he said that he felt its honors no more than if they had been offered to others; he gave audience to everybody, and the more lowly they were—especially the servants of God—the more willingly he heard them. He did not know the world through anger and vendetta, but with great mildness tolerated the whole world, which was very much against him with many slanders and persecutions. He said that when he suffered greater persecution, he felt God's greater sweetness all the more. He did not know the world through avarice, since he never granted benefices by simony, but only to able and virtuous persons, and he always sought God's honor. He did not know the world through envy, even though he received many insults from the envious, and he would say in all his troubles, "For my part, I have no enemies; every man has his opposite." He did not know the world through gluttony or through lust, since he was entirely sober and chaste; he neither ate nor slept unless he was hungry or very tired. He was adorned with all the virtues and therefore did not know the world, since he was crucified to the world and the world to him. And therefore he was persecuted by the world, because the world did not know him.

As an indication of this, when he passed from this life he appeared to his beloved Brother Matteo, who was at an abbey in Rimini where he lived alone among the savage beasts as he had long wanted to do. While he was in prayer, praying for the holy church, this glorious Gregory appeared and called to him, saying, "Oh Brother Matteo, I'm leaving." He asked, "Holy father, where are you going?" He said to him, "I'm going to the desert. Do you want to come with me?" Brother Matteo responded, "Not right now," and all at once Gregory vanished. This happened on Saint Luke's day at the hour of none; and so he wrote down the day and hour, and found that the blessed soul had passed away and appeared to Brother Matteo.[72] And as for his saying, "Do you want to come with me," he understood this in light of the affection they both had borne for the holy church, as if to mean, "What pastor shall come after me with as much concern for the honor of God and the holy church?"

To tell the truth, people like him are rare. To show just how rare they are, once when our father was discussing with a number of servants of God the exceptional virtues of many people, he came to the conclusion and said that of all

72. The feast of Saint Luke is October 18.

the servants of God that he had known personally, he had found only three who were complete in every virtue and perfection, and one of them was Pope Gregory XII. This was confirmed by all those who knew him and frequented him day and night, who said that he never remained idle: he always spoke of and discussed the holy Scriptures, no one dared speak ill of others in his presence, and he sharply reprimanded those who spoke idle words. Our father told us that he could never discover in him even a venial sin, so pure did he find him in confession. Therefore well might he say, "Who will follow after me now that I am departing from this vale of tears and going off to the desert?" That is, to life eternal, which is a true desert, devoid of all evil, of which the Lord Jesus Christ speaks in the holy Gospel about the shepherd who left the ninety-nine lambs in the desert and came down here to find the one that was lost.[73]

Another vision was seen by a woman in Recanati. While she was praying in the church where Gregory is buried, she saw visibly on his tomb a lovely little infant boy, very joyful, with a fine olive branch in his hand. She understood this to be the soul of Gregory, who rejoiced at the holy church's unity and peace, of which he, with his very great charity and humility, had been the origin. And God showed him in this way that it was his wish that he humble himself, for God wanted to give him the satisfaction of seeing the church united before he died. As he had often said, "I trust in my Lord Jesus Christ, that before I die I will see the holy church in peace and unity." He lived for two years after unity was restored. Day after day and month after month, they could never agree to elect one pope; they had come together there to create a pope and yet could never reach an agreement, so that those at the council were getting very frustrated. Once this saint died, the pope was elected twenty-four days after his death, which everyone held to be a great marvel of God to demonstrate that he was the true pope, since God would not allow another to be created so long as he was alive. When the news reached Lord Carlo of Rimini, he said, "I expected this to happen. Though they had to create a pope, I still thought that the Lord God would not permit it while he who had humbled himself by renouncing the papacy for his love was alive; and therefore he had the olive branch in his hand as a sign that he had gained the victory over his enemies and restored the church to peace."

Here I conclude the story of the many tribulations and the death of Pope Gregory XII, since I am sure that other people will write many wonderful things about his holy life and his perfect patience and his happy and holy death. But I wanted to say these few words in order that he might pray for me, a sinner.

73. Matt. 18:12–13; Luke 15:4–7.

THE NECROLOGY OF CORPUS DOMINI

I

HOW SISTER PAOLA ZORZI DIED IN THE FIRST YEAR THAT THE CONVENT WAS ENCLOSED

In the first year that the convent was enclosed, Sister Paola Zorzi passed from this life at the age of thirteen; she was the purest of virgins and adorned with every virtue. She was not yet professed. She was one of the women from San Girolamo.[1]

II

HOW SISTER CATERINA COSTANTINI DIED

In the year 1400 Sister Caterina Costantini died on April 4 at the hour of sext.[2] She was twenty years old and lived in the convent for five years, the purest of virgins and consecrated to the holy veil. She was of such humility that she never got upset over any chiding she received. She was very much given to prayer and weeping and received great consolation from the Lord Jesus Christ. Having received the holy sacraments, she rendered her soul to God on Saturday of the octave of Easter. She was among the women who entered that first day when the convent was enclosed. *Deo gratias.* Amen.

---

1. Although she shares the same name, this is obviously not the Paola Zorzi who was the mother of Giovanni Dominici. Since this Sister Paola had not yet reached the canonical age of consent at which she could pronounce final vows, she was still a novice. San Girolamo was a convent of Augustinian nuns in the same district of the city as Corpus Domini.

2. The fourth of the canonical hours of worship, at midday.

III

HOW SISTER GEROLAMA PASSED FROM THIS LIFE

In that same year, on May 4, Sister Gerolama Mercanti passed from this life, on Sunday at the hour of matins.[3] She was twenty-one years old and was one of the women from San Girolamo. She stayed in that convent for three years like a soul yearning to find perfection. She left the house of the servant and came to that of the Lord, where she lived for five years and was consecrated to the holy veil. She was of such perfection that no one ever heard a wicked word from her mouth, nor did she want to hear talk that was not about God. When the hour of her death approached, she had herself laid on the ground and stretched out her arms like a cross, tilted her head to the right side, and rendered her soul to her spouse Jesus Christ, who chose for himself this pure virgin.

IV

HOW SISTER MARINA OGNIBEN DIED

In that year Sister Marina Ogniben passed from this life on June 20 at the hour of compline.[4] She was twenty-two years old and had lived in the order for five years and was consecrated. She was a young woman of holy life and great fervor, and entered the convent with a younger sister, without the permission of her mother and her relatives. She fell sick and remained ill for a year, bearing it with very great patience. A few days before her death a voice was clearly audible singing very sweetly and devoutly in the infirmary where she lay ill, which one can only believe was some holy angel that came to visit the bride of Christ. When she received Communion she remained almost rapt from herself, with her face so joyous that it seemed to radiate light, and when she returned to herself she said to me, "I fear that the devil might stir some vanity in me, since when I saw my Lord come to visit me, I prepared to plunge myself entirely in God and to receive him so that he would receive me, and I could not contain myself so that it would not be apparent from the outside." I reassured her that she should not worry, since he in whom she had plunged herself would protect her, and so she remained happy, saying, "When shall I leave this prison? Oh,

3. The first office of the day, sung before dawn.
4. Compline, the last of the seven canonical hours of worship, is a brief service that follows the evening meal and closes the monastic day.

my Lord, receive me in you." When the hour of vespers drew near, she said, "Sisters, I am departing now; pray to God for me." And then she raised her eyes and said, "Accept our entreaties," and she rendered her soul to her beloved spouse the Lord Jesus Christ, who took for himself this pure virgin. *Deo gratias.* Amen.

V

HOW SISTER MARGARITA PIACENTINI DIED

In 1401 Sister Margarita Piacentini passed from this life on February 16 at the second hour of the night. She was a pure virgin and came the first day that the convent was enclosed with a sister who was younger than her, and she lived in the order for five years and was consecrated to the holy veil.[5] She was a young woman of such perfection and such observance [of the rule] that she never broke silence, and she would repeat the office until she thought that it had been said flawlessly. Now, she remained ill for fifteen months with such patience that it was amazing. The day before she passed away, while the sick woman was sleeping with her sister by her, the sister saw a round object more radiant than the sun at the feet of the sick woman and she called out to the sick woman in fear: it seemed as if all at once she woke up and opened her mouth and that light immediately entered the sick woman's mouth. From this one can see how acceptable that blessed soul was to her spouse, the Lord Jesus Christ. And having received the holy sacraments, she rendered her soul to God. *Deo gratias.* Amen.

VI

HOW SISTER CHIARA BUONIO DIED

In 1401 Sister Chiara Buonio passed from this life on the last day of March at the age of seventeen. She was a nun at Santa Caterina and stayed there for six years.[6] Seeing that the rule was not observed, she made arrangements with her mother, who was a spiritual woman, and entered this convent. She lived here for three years in very great desire for perfection, and out of humility she performed the most demeaning chores in the convent with the greatest joy. It

---

5. Her younger sister was Andreola: see the chronicle, chapter 5.

6. Santa Caterina was another convent of Augustinian nuns, situated (like San Girolamo) in the same section of the city as Corpus Domini.

pleased the Lord God to test her and give her an illness that lasted more than a year, and she accepted it as a gift of God. When death drew near, she was consecrated and with all the holy sacraments rendered her soul to her ardent spouse. *Deo gratias*. Amen.

VII

HOW SISTER MARIA RIZZI PASSED FROM THIS LIFE

In that year Sister Maria Rizzi passed from this life on April 12, a Sunday, at the hour of sext. She was twenty years old and a pure virgin. She was one of the women who entered on the first day the convent was enclosed, and she lived in the order for six years. She was a very obedient woman and remained ill for a long time. It pleased God to grant her rest; she received the holy sacraments and serenely rendered her soul to the celestial spouse.

VIII

HOW SISTER CATERINA ROSSO DIED

In 1401 Sister Caterina Rosso passed from this life on May 20. She was one of those seven women who came from the convent of San Girolamo. She was forty-one years old; she stayed at San Girolamo for twenty-one years, and she lived in this convent for seven years in such perfection that I am incapable of describing it, for she was a woman very much given to prayer and tears. Every seventh month she recited a psalter every night, not to mention the other prayers that she said unceasingly. She bore her illness patiently for six years, and before she died the Lord Jesus Christ appeared to her in the way she was often accustomed to see him and said to her, "Caterina, my daughter, would you like me to release you from this prison?" She replied saying, "My lord, I beg you to do so." She immediately ran a very high fever, and five days later, having received all the holy sacraments, she passed from this mortal life to eternal glory.

IX

HOW SISTER CRISTINA DIED

In that same year Sister Cristina dalla Terra passed from this life. She was fifty-five years old, a widow, and she came on the first day and lived in this convent for eight years, bearing constant illness with great patience. Thanking God, she passed from this false life. *Deo gratias.*

X

HOW SISTER FELICITAS BUONIO DIED

In 1403, on Saint Valentine's day, Sister Felicitas Buonio passed from this life at the age of eighteen years. She was a purest virgin in her thoughts, as she also demonstrated by her actions. She was so gentle and gracious that she seemed like an angel. She inspired devotion in whoever looked at her; her life was prayer with holy meditation and true observance and obedience. Once while she was in the choir during the octave of Corpus Christi, when the little door of the sacrament is kept open, she was looking at the host and saw there a lovely child who seemed to rejoice and promise her life eternal.[7] A few days later she fell sick and remained ill for a year; she was consecrated and received all the holy sacraments, and with highest devotion rendered her soul to her beloved spouse.

XI

HOW SISTER CATERINA SIMONI DIED

On July 19 of that same year Sister Caterina Simoni, known as Nona, passed from this life. She was twenty-two years old and had lived here for ten years. She was a pure virgin and was one of those who were enclosed the first day. She served all the sisters willingly, and when she was chided by one of them she strove to do better. When she had fallen ill and been consecrated, she received all the holy sacraments and rendered her soul to Christ.

XII

HOW SISTER MARUZZA BONZI DIED

In that year Sister Maruzza Bonzi, the mother of Sister Franceschina da Noale, passed from this life. She belonged to the Third Order of Saint Francis and

---

7. The octave is the eighth day, or period of eight days counting inclusively, following a liturgical festival. The feast of Corpus Christi is celebrated on the Thursday after Trinity Sunday (in effect, sixty days after Easter).

lived for nearly a hundred years.[8] She fell ill and was almost at the point of death, and out of respect for her daughter she was brought inside here and dressed in our holy habit, and she lived twenty-two days with great devotion. This blessed woman was like the good tree that bears good fruit, since her daughter Sister Franceschina and her two daughters and niece belong to our order, and the convent has more than two thousand ducats of her goods.[9] I believe that because of the good fruits that have sprung from her, she is enjoying the good things of life eternal. Amen.

XIII

HOW SISTER GIOVANNA DA LORETO DIED

In 1404 Sister Giovanna da Loreto passed from this life on March 11. She was a pure virgin of very great observance and penitence, given to vigils, prayer, flagellation, and tears, so that she fell ill and suffered from dropsy.[10] Despite all her infirmities, she struggled to do all that she could manage, so that it became necessary to order her not to strain herself so. She grew as thin as a crucifix. Her illness made her disgusting to look at, so that many were repulsed by her; and she bore it all with great patience, saying, "I deserve to be disdained; I am not worthy to be with these holy sisters." She struggled with this illness for six years, until it pleased the lord God to give his servant and spouse repose. While she was lying in bed gravely afflicted, the Lord Jesus Christ appeared to her and said, "Take comfort, daughter, for soon you shall come to rest with your spouse." Hearing this, she rose from bed and left the infirmary cell, saying, "My lord, I am not worthy to be your spouse or to enter such a beautiful

8. Members of the Third Order, or tertiaries, were laypeople affiliated with a religious order, though without pronouncing formal vows. Maruzza Bonzi's attachment to Saint Francis of Assisi is evident: not only did she become a Franciscan tertiary, but she named her daughter after Francis. Entering this Dominican convent at the end of her long life did not signify a break with the Franciscans: her testament stipulated the payment of a sum of money to each tertiary present at her funeral.

9. Her testament, dated April 21, 1403, says that she had been residing in Corpus Domini for three months (not the twenty-two days mentioned in the text). She bequeathed her main residence to her sons and left her female descendents in Corpus Domini the income from certain investments that were to revert to the convent after their deaths. Corpus Domini was also to receive her residual estate, after specific bequests had been paid. ASV, Corpus Domini, pergamene, busta 4: testament of Maruzza, widow of Biagio Bonzi, April 21, 1403.

10. Dropsy (or edema) is an unusual accumulation of fluid, causing swelling or bloating. This diagnosis is puzzling, since Sister Bartolomea remarks on how thin Giovanna was. Perhaps her ankles and feet were swollen by fluid retention caused by heart failure; or it may be that she had a bloated belly and emaciated limbs, the result of malnutrition caused by her penitential practices.

palace as the one you showed me." She was put to bed, and her brother (who belongs to our order) was summoned. He gave her the holy sacraments, and immediately after receiving unction, with great devotion she rendered her soul to her spouse. Her brother recited the office for her and buried her with great devotion. Amen.

XIV

HOW THE LAY SISTER SISTER AMBROSINA DIED

In 1405 the lay sister Sister Ambrosina, who had been with the order for nine years, passed from this life; she was thirty years old.[11] She was a woman of the greatest charity; she waited on all the sisters and did the vilest chores with the greatest satisfaction. She never left her devotions but went immediately to the church and stayed there very devoutly and with many tears. She was never heard to utter an idle word. As it pleased God, she fell sick with a very serious infirmity that lasted more than three years. Having received all the holy sacraments, as the hour of her death approached she saw the devil and began to cry, "What do you think you're doing, you wicked beast? I'm not afraid of you." Shortly thereafter she rendered her soul to her spouse.

XV

HOW SISTER DIAMANTE PASSED FROM THIS LIFE

In 1405 Sister Diamante died on March 24; she was twenty years old.[12] She was one of the women who entered on the first day the convent was enclosed. She was a good nun and a purest virgin; she always studied the Holy Scriptures and had an excellent mind for reading and singing and writing; she was very devout and had some great revelations from God. Sometimes she remained rapt in spirit for a day and a night without moving her body. She had a great longing for martyrdom: the lady Saint Ursula and all her companions ap-

11. A *conversa*, or lay sister, bore primary responsibility for the functioning of the convent rather than for choral prayer or worship. Lay sisters did not have the right to sit in chapter, but they enjoyed greater freedom of movement: they could leave the convent to tend the ill, for instance— or, as they did in 1476, to remove the relics of Saint Lucy from the nearby church of Santa Lucia.

12. Sister Diamante Mussolini (also known as Diamante dalle Carcere) was the subject of a letter from Giovanni Dominici about the struggle between the body and the soul. This letter was written September 20, 1400, when Diamante was just fifteen and had already been sick for two years. Dominici, *Lettere spirituali*, 139–40 (letter 23).

peared to her, and it was revealed to her that she would join that company.[13] Soon thereafter she fell sick with a terrible disease: she vomited a lot of blood with horrendous agony and without any remedy, with such tremors and fainting that it was a pity to see her. This blessed woman always maintained a joyous expression, with such patience that all the sisters marveled. When asked how she was, she replied, "I'm very well, since I am getting closer to going to my dear spouse." Despite this desire, God kept her ill for seven years, to show how he wanted to fulfill the promise that she would be part of the company of Saint Ursula, virgin and martyr. Having received all the holy sacraments, she rendered her soul to her spouse on the day of the Holy Trinity, a day she held in the highest reverence. She appeared to the woman who cared for her all lovely and adorned, and explained, "This beautiful adornment is the reward the Lord has given me for the illness that I patiently bore in this life," as if she possessed what in this world she had desired for so long.

XVI

HOW SISTER MUSSOLINI DIED

In 1406 Sister Margarita Mussolini passed from this life on March 26, at the age of thirty-four. A purest virgin, she was one of the women who entered the first day that the convent was enclosed. She was a good nun, very observant and obedient, and she delighted to stay in her cell. She was a woman of few words, and when she talked she spoke of the blessings and glory of paradise and of her sins. She considered herself a great sinner and delighted in hearing stories of the servants of God. Even if she sometimes went to the windows, she spoke of God with such fervor that everyone who heard her went away contrite and consoled, and this was because she didn't meddle in other people's business. She spent all the time that was left to her in prayer; she was very assiduous about choral worship and fulfilling her every obligation. When it pleased God to reward her labors, he sent her a serious illness that lasted a year. Then, having received all the sacraments and knowing the hour of her passing, she asked that the clapper be sounded so that everyone could be present at her death; and then she raised her hands to heaven and passed from this life at the

---

13. Saint Ursula was a Christian martyr who probably died in 303, during the persecution of Diocletian. A tenth-century account of her martyrdom made her the daughter of the king of Britain, killed at Cologne by the Huns along with her eleven thousand virgin companions. Devotion to Saint Ursula was deeply rooted in Venice: toward the end of the fifteenth century, the Venetian artist Carpaccio did a striking series of paintings (now in the Accademia) depicting the legend of Saint Ursula.

third hour of the night.[14] Some of the sisters went back to sleep after she had passed away, and at that instant this blessed soul appeared to them with great joy. She clarified some things they had wondered about and said that God pays less heed to the external act than to interior love. Another sister saw a great multitude of white angels at the hour of her passing, among which were three large, gleaming white ones that preceded the rest to the sick woman's cell. When she marveled at this, she was informed that the three who led the way were Saint Dominic, Saint Peter Martyr, and Saint Thomas Aquinas, who had come with the whole order of holy preachers to accompany that soul to the glory of paradise, since she had borne such affection for the order.[15]

XVII

HOW SISTER FRANCESCHINA DA NOALE DIED

Sister Franceschina da Noale entered the convent seven days after it was enclosed, as a widowed lady forty-nine years old. During her marriage she lived in the world in a holy fashion and always wore a hair shirt under her velvet. When she was left a widow she dressed humbly in coarse cloth; and when this convent was built, moved by desire for greater perfection she came to the order, bringing with her a seven-year-old daughter. This blessed woman never meddled with her daughter, who was entrusted to the care of the [novice] mistress. Her own life was a constant round of prayers, vigils, flagellation, fasts, and other holy deeds, such that she fell ill and consumed that body, which did not have the appearance of a living thing. She bore this infirmity with the greatest patience for a long time. When it pleased God, she received all the holy sacraments and serenely rendered her soul to God. Amen.

XVIII

HOW SISTER DOMENICA DIED

On the day of Saint Martha [July 29], Sister Domenica Moro died. After the death of her mother this blessed woman resided with a brother of hers, with the intention of not marrying; and she lived with her brother like this for five

---

14. During periods when silence was observed in the convent, a wooden clapper was used to summon the sisters in place of the more resonant bell.

15. This vision features the three principal saints of the Dominican order: its founder, its first martyr, and its greatest scholar.

years, a purest virgin. When this convent was built, she offered herself to the convent together with her brother, who stayed on as a servant and worked for the women for many years, living in a holy fashion. The sister entered and acted as everyone's mother, serving both healthy and sick with great charity. At table she never ate anything good but took the worst bread and the worst things and gave the good to her companions. All her words were humble and patient. She considered herself unworthy of any good thing, and since she wanted to serve the sisters she asked the Lord for the favor of not sending her a long illness. God granted that she always stayed healthy until a fever struck her fifteen days before her death; and when the hour of her passing came, her face began to brighten and she said, "May the Holy Trinity be welcome; blessed be the Incarnate Word in Mary's womb." And having received all the holy sacraments, she passed from this miserable life.

XIX

HOW SISTER CRISTINA CORNARO DIED

In 1408 Sister Cristina Cornaro passed from this life on March 11; she had lived in the order for thirteen years, and she was thirty-six years old. She was a pure virgin and very observant, zealous for the honor of God and the order, and full of charity for all the sisters. She was sick for a year but made every effort not to stay in the infirmary so as not to give the sisters any trouble. However, six days before she passed away her illness grew so severe that she could not get out of bed, and so she was given all the sacraments at the second hour of the night. She received them with great devotion and tears, saying, "My Lord, I am not worthy to have you enter into a sinner like me. I give myself entirely unto you; do with me what you will." And shortly thereafter she stretched out and said that she wanted to sleep. At the fifth hour of the night the clapper was sounded, and the sisters had barely arrived there when this blessed soul expired, almost with the sacrament in her mouth; and I think that God granted this because she had taken such joy in frequent Communion.

XX

HOW SISTER LUCIA FAGIUOLI DIED

On January 15 of that same year Sister Lucia Fagiuoli passed from this life. She was a widow who came to the order with great fervor and lived for twelve years. She was very observant and obedient, humble and patient, kind and full of good deeds—so much so that when she fell ill and remained ill for five years, she still strove to do all that she could. God wanted to reward her for her good works by aggravating her illness; and having received the holy sacraments in good spirits she passed from this life at the age of forty years.

XXI

HOW SISTER LUCIA CANAL DIED

In 1410 Sister Lucia Canal passed from this life on January 9. She had lived in the order for fourteen years. She was twenty-eight years old, a virgin pure in mind and body, and she loved virginity so much that she used to say that she would rather suffer a thousand martyrdoms than have the slightest thought contrary to virginity, and all her studies were devoted to reading legends of holy virgins and every scripture that spoke of this virtue. To test her, I said to her on various occasions, "Beware of pride, because you display such pleasure over this virginity." And she answered me, "I truly can't help it, because I feel such an abundance of joy and satisfaction that God has not allowed me to take a husband and instead has taken me for his bride; and the more I think about it, the more humbled I feel in my mind." She was also truly obedient; she did not wait for the superior's instructions, but as soon as she realized that something needed to be done, she was the first to run to obey. She also wanted to be poor, saying, "I would rather have a demon in my cell than a shilling." She wanted nothing more than the barest necessities. One could truly say that this holy woman observed perfectly the three principal vows that sum up the entire substance of the religious life.[16] She never missed coming to the office because of lingering at the windows or for any other thing she might have to do, except when obedience constrained her; and when her relatives visited her, she sent them away as soon as she could. Her father, mother, brothers, and sisters died, and she was never seen to weep. Her mother and sisters were buried in here with us; she did not stir to touch them but sang with the rest just as if they had no connection with her. She acted as if she were worthless and cared little for the world's honor. All her efforts were directed at toiling diligently for the convent, so that she grew so weak that she remained in bed for five years, getting up only when the convent received Communion. Then she had two sisters carry her like a lump into church, where she confessed and received Communion along with the others with the greatest devotion. Thus she bore her infirmities patiently until the Lord saw fit to grant her rest. As her illness worsened,

---

16. That is, poverty, chastity, and obedience.

she received all the holy sacraments and rendered her soul to her beloved spouse whom she had greatly desired for a long time.

XXII

HOW SISTER FRANCESCHINA DELLO ABATE DIED

In 1411 Sister Franceschina,[17] who had lived in the order for fifteen years, passed from this life; she died on December 8. She was a widowed woman, and one of those who entered the first day the convent was enclosed. She was more than seventy years old and was an observant woman and full of holy deeds. She remained ill for one year with great patience and received all the holy sacraments, then rendered her soul to God.

XXIII

HOW THE VICARESS SISTER MARGARITA PARUTA DIED

On July 18, 1412, Sister Margarita Paruta passed from this life. She was a widowed woman, and she and her husband Messer Marco Paruta were a great help in renovating this convent. After the convent was enclosed she remained in the world for three and a half years. When her husband died she offered herself to the order, giving both herself and all her possessions, which amounted to more than two thousand ducats.[18] She was as poor, obedient, and submissive as any of the least of the sisters, and so wise and discreet that she was deservedly chosen as vicaress; and because the prioress was very old and ill, she ran the convent.[19] This blessed woman strove to have everyone maintain the good practices of the convent and live ceremoniously. She also liked the convent to have books and everything it needed, and with the help of her family and friends she had altar cloths and surplices made. She also used her resources to purchase the vineyard and have windows opened in the cells, which had been all sealed because people passing by in the street could see in, and so the cells never had any air, though the rafters had a round glass window that let in a little light; and things remained like this for more than four years. She also

17. Sister Franceschina presumably received her surname because she was the mother of the abbot of San Giorgio: chronicle, chapter 5.
18. She had entered the convent by July 23, 1397, when her name appears in a list of the sisters: Dominici, *Lettere spirituali*, 347.
19. She replaced the first vicaress, Lucia Dandolo.

built the new parlor and the old granary with all those sheds, and she made the cloister and many other things the convent needed. She finished her life still striving to do good deeds. She remained infirm for three years, so feeble that she had to be carried around the convent in our arms. She begged the sisters to relieve her [of her office], but they never wished to do so because all the women thought the convent would suffer great harm if it were deprived of her governance. And so she lived for ten years in this office with great patience, and she received all the holy sacraments and rendered her soul to God. *Deo gratias.*

XXIV

HOW THE PRIORESS SISTER LUCIA TIEPOLO DIED

On April 12, 1413, Sister Lucia Tiepolo, prioress of the convent, passed from this life. She was the one who gave the little church its start in the manner re-counted earlier.[20] At first she was a nun in the order of Saint Benedict; she took that habit at the age of eleven and lived in that order for more than eighty years; then, at the hands of our father, she was clothed in our habit and was one of the women who entered on the first day. She lived humbly and acted patiently and charitably toward all, observing [the rule] and working for as long as she could; and she was especially dedicated to choral prayer, remaining there very de-voutly and weeping profusely. It was an inspiration to see a woman so old make such great efforts. Her face was always joyous, and from the moment she was en-closed she never wanted to see a man's face. When doctors or teachers came, she fled; sometimes she could not escape quickly enough on account of her old age, and so she covered her face with her scapular. The young women asked her, "Why do you flee like this?" She replied, "My dear daughters, even now I fear for my virginity. The vicaress and doorkeepers can manage without me."

She was very devout and much given to prayer. During the war [against Padua] she prayed with tremendous weeping and sighing day and night, such that she was heard to cry out, and some of the sisters went there thinking that she needed something. Finding that she did not want anything, they pressed her to explain why she had cried with so many tears and sighs. She answered them privately, saying, "My dear daughters, our Lord God is greatly offended. All the war's tribulations are due to the great sins of the world. I pray that he may give victory to this state, and he replies to me that *non in armis sed in precibus,* so that, dear daughters, you should be fervent in your prayers if you want this city to be victorious." So it was that our forces marvelously entered Padua

20. This suggests that at least the earlier portion of the chronicle was written before this entry.

without arms and gained the victory.[21] And this blessed woman also said that the church would suffer great tribulation and persecution, but that it would turn out well in the end.

One could recount many noteworthy things that the Lord performed by divine grace in this his handmaiden, which I will leave out for reasons of brevity—though I will report one small one. When one of our sisters was in prayer, one of our dead appeared to her; and the living sister asked the dead one many things, to which she replied. Finally, the living one asked the dead, "Please tell me, which of the women in this convent is most acceptable to God?" The dead one replied, "The prioress." "Why?" asked the living one, and the dead replied, "For her great humility." She was the sort of person who was satisfied with anything and did not want to trouble anyone who was staying by her, though she had great need, especially at night. She was always found in prayer and was never heard to complain. She had attained such purity that she seemed like a little child. She always had a joyous expression and always yearned to be united with her spouse, who was pleased to fulfill her long-standing desire, since she lived more than a hundred years. She was an extremely healthy woman. Now, five days before her death, having said vespers and remained in prayer with her rosary in her hands, she lost her speech, and the rosary could never again be pried from her grasp. She passed so sweetly from this life that one may recognize how much her prayers had pleased God during her life, if even in death she seemed to be praying. An even more amazing thing was that her body remained as white as snow and so smooth that she seemed like a girl.[22] From this we can learn how much her purity had pleased her most beloved and celestial spouse.

XXV

HOW SISTER CHIARA MARIN DIED

In 1414 Sister Chiara Marin passed from this life on February 12. She was one of the women who came from San Girolamo, and she lived in the order for eighteen years and six months. She was thirty-seven years old, a purest virgin,

---

21. Padua submitted to Venice in November 1405. The sentiment that victory is won not with arms but with prayers echoes 2 Cor. 10:3–4: "For though we live in the world we are not carrying on a worldly war, for the weapons of our warfare are not worldly but have divine power to destroy strongholds."

22. This is a commonplace in the lives of female saints. For some examples, see Gabriella Zarri, "Living Saints: A Typology of Female Sanctity in the Early Sixteenth Century," in *Women and Religion in Medieval and Renaissance Italy,* ed. Daniel Bornstein and Roberto Rusconi (Chicago: University of Chicago Press, 1996), 286 n. 117.

full of charity, fervent in prayer with weeping. She performed all that our holy order commands for as long as she could. She remained ill for a long time; and having received all the holy sacraments, with great devotion she rendered her soul to God. *Deo gratias.*

XXVI

HOW SISTER ANDREOLA PIACENTINI DIED

In that same year Sister Andreola Piacentini passed from this life. She was one of the women who were enclosed on the first day, along with one of her sisters, and she was a purest virgin. She was very observant and a willing servant of all. She fell ill and remained sick for more than two years. She prayed the Lord God that he would grant her this grace: that when it pleased him to take her from this life, he would do so on the day of Communion so that she could not commit any more sins. But the kindly and glorious God, who welcomes good desires, wished to satisfy his beloved spouse; and even though she received Communion and unction many times, believing that she was about to die, finally, feeling afflicted, she herself asked to confess on March 8. The prior was sent for, and she confessed and received Communion with great fervor and then crossed her hands on her breast. The woman who tended her asked, "Daughter, would you like a little broth?" "No, mother," she replied; and before the hour was out the clapper was sounded and all the sisters ran to find her with her hands in the form of a cross and her face joyous and tranquil. She seemed like an angel, so sweetly had she expired. *Deo gratias.*

XXVII

HOW THE MOTHER OF THE LORD CARDINAL DIED

In 1416 Sister Paola, who was the mother of our venerable father the lord cardinal, passed from this life. When this blessed woman was left a widow, she was a seventeen-year-old girl—seventeen, I tell you. She lived very properly with her three children, two of whom died before long, leaving just this one. She let him enter the order of preaching friars as he wished, while she busied herself continually in works of mercy, giving both of her goods and her person, especially to the poor friars of the order. She came to be known as the mother of the poor, and everyone held her in great respect.

When her blessed son had built our convent, he wanted his mother to come cloister herself for love of God; and she humbly obeyed, making herself poor. She gave all she had and her own self into the hands of holy obedience, in which obedience she always strove to be first, performing the vilest chores, never tiring of staying with the sick day and night and even serving the healthy. She never dreamed of honors or of going about well dressed; she was never seen to preen with pleasure at her son's honors, just as she never grew sad over his troubles, though he often risked death to defend the holy church. When the sisters comforted her, with a cheerful expression she replied, "Dear daughters, you can be sure that I feel no anguish, considering that he is toiling for God's honor; and if I should hear that he was killed while defending the holy church, I would feel the highest joy, for he would make me out to be the mother of a martyr."

She was also very patient in her long infirmity. She accepted everything, always thanking God and saying, "May my Lord God be ever thanked for the many good things he has done for me, miserable and deserving of damnation." When she was afflicted with illness, she felt no relief except when her bed was made; and she never wanted it to be prepared on Fridays, out of reverence for the Passion. She would say, "On that day my Lord suffered for my sins the agony of the cross without any relief, and so I don't want any either." Similarly, on that day she never wished to eat soup, out of reverence for the sponge that was given to Christ.

For brevity's sake, I shall omit many things that might be said of this blessed woman. Now, when the end of her life drew near, she received with great fervor all the holy sacraments on March 2. She lost her speech while saying the Hail Mary: she went for four days without taking any food, and during those days she did not speak, though she maintained a joyous expression as if she were in contemplation, and she often laughed while she lay dying. Thus in good spirits she passed from this miserable life to life eternal at the hour of none. She was buried with very great lamenting not only on the part of the sisters, but also of the friars, who gave her a lovely and devout funeral with a pious sermon. The abbot of San Giorgio and many other servants of God and some devout gentlemen were present, along with a lot of other people, and everyone mourned out of respect for her son.[23] One servant of God was cele-

23. The abbot of San Giorgio Maggiore, Giovanni Michiel, was a close friend of Tommaso Tommasini and other members of the circle of Giovanni Dominici. Under their influence, he was inspired to undertake a reform of his abbey, restoring the strict observance of the Benedictine rule. See Paolo Sambin, "L'abate Giovanni Michiel (†1430) e la riforma di S. Giorgio Maggiore di Venezia," in *Miscellanea Gilles Gerard Meersseman,* Italia Sacra 15–16 (Rome: Herder, 1970), 483–545. Since Giovanni Michiel's mother was Giovanna Bragadin, he cannot be the abbot of San Giorgio whose mother, Franceschina dello Abate, had died in 1411 after fifteen years as a sister in Corpus Domini: chronicle, chapter 5; necrology, chapter 22.

brating mass in his church when he was told in spirit, "Hurry to Corpus Domini." When he finished the mass he said, "Something must really have happened at that convent"; he rushed over and found that the sermon was being preached. He inquired and was told how the monsignor's mother had passed from this life: he thanked God for making him worthy of being present at the funeral of such a holy woman and received great consolation. One may gather from this how acceptable she was to God while living, if in her death she inspired such devotion. She was fifty-eight years old when she entered the religious life, and she lived for another twenty-two years. The prioress wrote on behalf of our convent to our father, who was at the council to bring peace to the church, lamenting the loss of such a pillar as his mother; and he wrote a beautiful and devout letter to comfort us.[24] *Deo gratias.*

XXVIII

HOW SISTER MARUZZA CONTARINI DIED

In 1417 Sister Maruzza Contarini passed from this life on September 1, at the hour of compline. She was the prioress's companion and came the first day the convent was enclosed. Her relatives had made her a nun at Santa Maria degli Angeli at the age of seven, and she came here when she was fifty-seven and lived here for twenty-two years and two months.[25] Among her other virtues, she was very dedicated to choral prayer. She was so accustomed to it that when she was so old that she had lost her sight, all her physical strength, and much of her intellect, the only pleasure she had left was the divine office. As feeble and infirm as she was, when she heard it sounded there was no one who could hold her back: she steadied herself with her cane and hurried off to the choir. She kept this up until three days before she passed on, and having received the holy sacraments she expired peacefully.

The Lord God then performed a marvelous thing. The night that she passed on, she appeared to her brother-in-law, the husband of one of her sisters, who is a respectable man, a medical doctor who comes to treat our sisters for the love of God. He came one morning earlier than usual; when he was told that his sister-in-law had died, he replied, "I knew that before anyone told me of it" and proceeded to recount how he had seen a lovely vision that moved

---

24. The Council of Constance, which Giovanni Dominici attended as the representative of Gregory XII. This letter is not found in Dominici, *Lettere spirituali.*

25. Santa Maria degli Angeli was a convent of Augustinian nuns on the island of Murano, in the Venetian lagoon.

him to great devotion. He begged the prioress to be so kind as to allow him to see her, and to grant him that pleasure the prioress led him into the church where the corpse lay. When he saw her he began to weep and sigh. The vision that he had seen went like this: his wife woke up and said, "My lord, last night I saw a great multitude of people elaborately arrayed. I'm still completely bewildered and have no idea what this might mean." Master Bartolomeo said, "I saw the same sort of thing tonight. It seemed to me that I was near a church around which there was a great multitude of fine people, all properly dressed and adorned to enter that church; and I went in with them right up to the altar. Around the altar were set multitudes of large candles. When I wondered about these solemnities, I was informed, 'This is the funeral of your sister-in-law.' I turned to look at her and saw around her corpse the twelve most beautiful women I have ever seen, all dressed in purest gold; each of them had twelve golden stoles wrapped crosswise one on top of the other right up to their necks, so that only a bit of the face remained visible. I was awestruck by such beauty; I was told that this was how those who live in purity of mind and body for love of God are adorned."

One of the sisters had another vision. While praying in choir that day, in a sort of ecstasy she seemed to see a lovely convent, in which she saw some sisters who had passed from this life, including Sister Maruzza. She was told, "Know that only those who love God perfectly, like Sister Maruzza, can enter here. When her soul left her body, the Father Eternal received it in his arms." *Deo gratias.*

XXIX

HOW SISTER GABRIELLA OF SIENA DIED

In 1419 Sister Gabriella of Siena passed from this life on February 13 at the hour of none in great mental jubilation, saying, "I feel the pleasures of paradise, since my Lord Jesus Christ is here with me." The sisters comforted her, but she said in reply, "I am not suffering in the least. He can hold onto me as long as he wants, for I know that he is my spouse. When I was a little girl he gave me the ring, and I never knew anything of the flesh. I am so firm in the holy faith that I would suffer martyrdom if it were necessary; my Lord took a leap for me and I made one for him, and thus I trust firmly in him because he is my dear spouse." She said these words at terce, and at the hour of none she expired.[26] Her spirit left her so gently that it was a great comfort to all of us and also to the confes-

---

26. Terce was celebrated at midmorning, about 9:00; none was midafternoon, about 3:00.

sors who happened to be present, Brother Piero Contarini, priest and prior of San Zanipolo, and Brother Francesco of Bologna; they had stopped by the day before to give us all the holy sacraments, and they returned that day to communicate Sister Andreola Paruta, who was very sick. The leap that she made was this: with great fervor she had abandoned her father, mother, brothers, and sisters, and her own city, in order to come serve God in this convent. When our father was preaching in Siena before he was made a cardinal, he spoke at length of this convent; this woman was inspired to come, against her family's wishes. She was twenty-six years old when she came, and she lived fourteen years and ten months, for most of which she was ill. At the end she lay for sixteen days with a constant fever and went to her heavenly spouse a purest virgin.

XXX

HOW SISTER ANDREOLA TOMMASINI DIED

Ten days later, Sister Andreola Tommasini passed from this life after a continuous fever that lasted sixteen days. She was the woman who had this convent built, which she entered at the age of eleven and where she continued in holy observance for twenty-four years and eight months. She was adorned with all the virtues; she knew how to read and sing perfectly and was assiduous in performing the holy office and all other obligations. She was among the first and never spared herself, and even though she was among the leading women in the order, she took the place of the least out of humility. When the Lord decided to grant repose to her as his dearest and purest virgin spouse, she passed away on a Wednesday at the third hour of the night, having received all the holy sacraments, and she was buried the Thursday that the office of the Precious Sacrament is sung, to indicate that she had been responsible for building the convent dedicated to his body and to its reverence. And so, on the day that the Body of the Spouse is celebrated, the body of his beloved spouse was buried. To show that this is true, on the third day before she expired, one of the sisters dozed off after matins while thinking of her, and all at once she seemed to see a tree laden with gorgeous fruit being carried into our church with elaborate festivities, which caused her to marvel greatly. She was informed that this tree was the soul of Sister Andreola, which would be presented in the presence of her spouse full of many virtues. As soon as she awoke, she said to the woman who took care of her, "Truly, Sister Andreola will go to paradise on Thursday." And thus it was that she passed away with great devotion, and with great devotion she was buried that very Thursday.

XXXI

HOW OUR REVEREND FATHER DIED

On June 10, 1419, our reverend father Brother Giovanni Dominici, founder and father of this convent, passed from this life. After he had enclosed it, he remained in this city for five and a half years. As I have said, Pope Gregory made him his cardinal, and in his service he lived in constant company with the many troubles and tribulations and persecutions that he suffered for the holy church and the defense of the truth. Because he accepted this position of authority within the holy church not for pomp or profit but out of obedience, God promised that for his obedient service to the holy church he would die in conformity with Lord Jesus Christ, who in human form was obedient *usque ad mortem*.[27] Thus it happened that when unity had been restored to the holy church, a terrible heresy arose in the region of Bohemia which held that monks could marry and that the sacrament of the altar was not real; and many monks and nuns were killed by these wicked heretics for refusing to accept this perverse heresy.[28] After Pope Gregory died and Pope Martin V was elected pope by agreement of the entire council, everyone concurred that our father, as the wisest and most fervent zealot for God's honor, should be sent to extirpate that heresy, and he was made a legate with full authority to act on the pope's behalf. He went obediently, and when he had arrived in those areas of Bohemia he began to preach to lead those souls back to the true light. He wore himself out in preaching, lecturing, and debating, until finally he was stricken with pain in the sides and kidney stones, which had given him trouble in the past. And so the Lord saw fit to grant him repose, and he passed from this life serenely, full of good works and with a good reputation.

When the news reached our convent, everyone felt inexpressible sorrow at being deprived of such a venerable father, for even when he was far away physically he still continually visited us spiritually with his prayers and letters and epistles, urging us always to act well. He also solicited from Popes

27. Phil. 2:8: "And being found in human form he humbled himself and became obedient unto death, even death on a cross."

28. The Hussite heresy rejected papal authority, grounded doctrine in Scripture alone, and maintained that laypeople as well as priests could receive Communion in both kinds, wine as well as wafer. In the late fourteenth and early fifteenth centuries it attracted widespread support from both nobles and the populace in Bohemia, as an expression of Czech cultural and political identity. In July 1418 Pope Martin V sent Giovanni Dominici as his legate to Sigismund and Wenceslaus of Bohemia, charged with urging them to undertake a crusade against this heresy. His mission met with little success, and Giovanni retired to the Dominican friary of Buda, where he died on June 10, 1419.

Gregory and Martin a pardon on the Assumption valid forever for all the sisters in the convent, on condition that when first vespers is said they recite *Veni creator spiritus* and the seven psalms, and those who are too sick to come to choir should have the cross carried to them so that they might kiss it three times and receive the pardon. He also solicited a plenary indulgence *in articulo mortis* granting, for the space of a year, remission of sin and suffering to those sisters then living who chose to confess on any day they pleased and performed whatever penance the confessor saw fit to impose, thereby receiving this pardon. What is more, he bestowed upon his daughters not only spiritual goods, but temporal ones as well. Thus it was through his intervention that Pope Gregory instructed the prior of the Carceri in Padua to give our convent, out of his revenues, 100 ducats a year for fifteen years in a row.[29] In addition, even when he did not receive his revenues on account of the war and schism in the church, he still managed to send us a hundred bushels of grain and 100 ducats; and if he had lived three years longer, he would have endowed the convent as he wished.

He had the greatest affection for his daughters, which he demonstrated in life and in death. Once he wrote to inquire how many of the women he had left here were still alive and how many had died and how many there were at that moment, and he asked that each send him a ginger root as a sign of charity. When his daughters heard this, with the greatest joy they all searched to find a fine ginger root. Each one's name was written on a tag tied to her root, and one was put in a sack for each of the sixty-three sisters then in the convent. When he was presented with the sack, he sat down on a bench and opened it and emptied it, and while reading the names of his beloved daughters he could not hold back his tears, so that those who were present there were moved to weep at the sight of his humanity and sweetness. He wrote back that he welcomed the little ones no less than the big, since he saw that the charity of all was great; and he urged us all to act well and live in common. After his death, he left us all his silver, which we sold for 600 ducats and used the money to buy state bonds.[30]

Whoever tried to record everything that we saw and felt of his affectionate charity toward us would have a lot to write; but I will tell about one wonderful example of his charity for all. Just as the master of true charity loved all his disciples yet among them John was especially beloved, so our father felt, four years after it was enclosed, about those two beloved women who gave our

---

29. The prior evidently did not welcome this burden on his revenues and had to be reminded repeatedly of his obligation: ASV, Corpus Domini, pergamene, busta 6: letter of Antonio, bishop of Brescia, to the prior of the abbey of Santa Maria delle Carceri in the diocese of Padua; April 12, 1409. In 1420 Pope Martin V instructed the bishop of Treviso to settle the dispute between Corpus Domini and Santa Maria delle Carceri: ASV, Corpus Domini, pergamene, busta 6: letter of Martin V to the bishop of Treviso, June 17, 1420.

30. Shares in the public debt of Venice were a common form of investment by religious institutions, since they guaranteed a steady income.

convent its start. When our father learned that Sister Andreola, who was one of these two sisters, was sick and in very bad shape, he said, "When Sister Andreola dies, I will follow soon after her." We asked him why, and he replied, "Because we promised each other that whichever of us died first would ask the Lord God to allow the other to follow right away." And so it happened, since he lived just three months and three days after the death of Sister Andreola.

He had solicited two other privileges for his daughters. The first was that those who had received the habit from his hands would be spared the torments of hell—and he vested seventy women in this convent in the five and a half years that he resided in Venice [after the founding of the convent]. The second was that none of the women he vested would die of plague; and this we have found by experience to have come true, by the grace of the Lord Jesus Christ. He obtained this favor from God in the following way: two years after he enclosed the convent, the plague struck one of the sisters. Our father was immediately summoned to come and give her the sacraments; he replied that he would come in the morning. When he arrived the following morning he said, "There is no need for me to come inside. Don't worry, for she will not die from this illness." On the third day, she was safe and sound. He stopped by another day to rejoice with us over that sister's recovery and said, "Dear daughters, be of good spirits, since none of you will ever again have this disease; my Lord God has made me this promise."

In many such ways we have found by experience that our dear father is God's friend and has obtained many favors from his majesty on our behalf. No one who sought him out was so troubled and tempted that she did not depart consoled; whenever anything was needed, everyone went to him, and with great charity he provided for us all according to our needs. During the five and a half years that he stayed in this city we were like good infants hanging at their mother's breast, and when he left we lost a great comfort and spiritual and temporal support. Whoever wants to tell his life's story would have to be a wise and learned person, since I truly believe that he is a saint in celestial glory. Nonetheless, in my own little way I will say something about him.

HOW HE ENTERED THE ORDER, AND ABOUT HIS HOLY LIFE

This most holy man was from the city of Florence, the son of parents who were thoroughly honest and good in worldly terms.[31] His father was named Dominic and practiced the silk trade, and his mother was named Paola—and

---

31. For Giovanni's biography, see Stefano Orlandi, *Necrologio di S. Maria Novella, 1235–1504* (Florence: Olschki, 1955), 2:77–126; Giorgio Cracco, "Giovanni di Domenico Banchini," *Dizionario biografico degli italiani*, vol. 5 (Rome, 1963), 657–64.

he fully lived up to his parents' names, since he became a son of Saint Dominic, following the preachings of Saint Paul. His venerable mother told how she was left pregnant with him when his father died. When he was born, she named him Giovanni. He wanted to enter the order when he was fourteen years old, but his mother feared that the friars in Florence would not accept him, so she sent him off to Venice with a respectable merchant. While residing there in obedience to his mother, his good desire increased. He often visited San Zanipolo, and when the sermon was over he would climb into the pulpit and say, "Someday I shall see many people in this church at my sermons"—and so it came to pass. After two years had gone by his mother thought that he had gotten over the fervor to be a friar, so she sent for him; and as soon as he arrived in Florence he donned the habit of Saint Dominic in the friary of Santa Maria Novella.[32] His mother knew nothing, but as she waited for him at home and he did not appear, she thought of the kind of person he was and went off to Santa Maria Novella and asked for her son. When Brother Giovanni heard that his mother was looking for him, he said to the prior, "Let me speak with her, since I hope to God that I can leave her satisfied." The prior agreed and accompanied him into the church. When his mother saw him she was stricken with anguish, and when she came to herself she said, "My son, how can you take this habit and deprive your mother of her only son?" The son, seeing his mother lamenting greatly in such bitterness, said to her with great compassion, "Don't be upset, mother, for I still trust that my Lord, who has selected me for this holy order, will grant you the grace of being well pleased with me," and many other fine words. The prior too comforted her in similar terms, so that she went away consoled.

With my feeble talents, I could not recount his fine beginnings and how his obedience, poverty, chastity, and other virtues made him a good example to everyone. He was sent to Paris soon thereafter and returned full of great learning. He said that he had always longed to convert many souls to God but doubted that he could be understood because he stuttered. Hearing of the virtues of Saint Catherine of Siena, who died about that time and performed some great miracles, he appealed to her that he might be understood; and he received from her that grace so that in his day there was no preacher more outstanding.[33] He produced good fruits in every city he went to, especially

32. Giovanni Dominici probably entered the Dominican order about 1373. He was ordained a priest in 1380, became subprior of Santa Maria Novella in 1381, and in 1385–87 held the post of prior.

33. He himself described this miracle in a letter to the committee charged with her canonization proceedings: *Il Processo Castellano*, ed. Marie-Hyacinthe Laurent, Fontes Vitae S. Catharinae Senensis Historici 9 (Milan: Fratelli Bocca, 1942), 446–47.

Venice. He was not yet thirty years old when he was sent to San Zanipolo as lector; he spoke so effectively that he spread profound peace where there had been the most tremendous strife.[34] Whoever was troubled and tempted would go to him, and all would leave consoled. He converted many people in Venice during this period: upon hearing his sermons, merchants abandoned their crooked practices, the greedy gave alms, the dissolute became chaste. In short, he uprooted many vices from this city. Many people would not do anything at all without his advice. He gave such consolation and comfort to all during the twelve years he stayed in this city, as lector and as preacher at the government's request, that the Holy Spirit seemed to speak through him.

He was much beloved by everyone. He restored unity and peace between the Franciscans and Dominicans: he arranged that on the feast of Saint Francis all the Dominican friars would go as a group to hear the office and preach there, and the Franciscans responded in kind on the feast of Saint Dominic. He was so zealous for unity and peace that he bore some fruit in whatever city or place he visited. He brought the friars of San Zanipolo back to true obedience, so that those who did not want to observe the rule wanted to kill him. When his daughters learned of this, they prayed heartily for him. One in particular insisted with many tears that Lord Jesus Christ rescue him from these wicked men; she got an answer from the Holy Spirit, who said, "Don't worry, for I have sent the patriarchs Abraham, Isaac, and Jacob to watch over and protect him." And he truly was well protected by these three patriarchs, since San Zanipolo maintained the proper observance for more than thirteen years, while in this city alone, on more than seven occasions he was in danger of being killed for the salvation of souls. For he followed in the steps of Lord Jesus Christ, who said, "I have not come to bring peace on earth but a sword, and to set sons against their father."[35] Many men and women left their relatives and their children to become friars and nuns, and for this reason their relatives grew angry with him, saying, "This traitor is leading our children astray; let us remove him from the world." They got it into their heads to kill him when he came to say mass; but when one tried to lift his dagger his hand was held back and he could not harm the man of God, who was protected by those three patriarchs because he sought God's honor and the salvation of souls. When these people witnessed this miracle, they converted and became his dearest friends.

This holy man also restored the regular obedience in the friaries of San

---

34. He returned to Venice in 1388 and remained there until his expulsion in November 1399.

35. Matt. 10:34–35. On the tension between familial and spiritual obligations in this era of demographic disaster, see Daniel Bornstein, "Spiritual Kinship and Domestic Devotions," in *Gender and Society in Renaissance Italy,* ed. Judith C. Brown and Robert C. Davis (London: Addison Wesley Longman, 1998), 173–92.

Domenico in Venice and Chioggia, in Città di Castello and in Cortona, and
the one in Fiesole near Florence.[36] In short, he gave aid and counsel to all those
who wanted to live well. His advice and his sermons were so gentle and full of
wisdom that no one who heard them could deny their truth. In every city
where he sowed the word of God, he reaped an abundant harvest. He
preached twice a day during Lent and three or four times a day on holidays: in
the morning he went wherever he was invited; after lunch, at San Zanipolo;
the third time, here with us; and then he went to the palace to preach for the
doge's wife. The people who followed him around, both men and women, all
marveled that he could draw four sermons from a single gospel passage, each
one different from the others and all of them beautiful; but his mind was full of
natural intelligence and wisdom, and he had little need to study. All those who
knew him—popes, cardinals, bishops, friars, and secular clergy—said they
had never heard a man with such a memory, prudence, and eloquence in the
Holy Scriptures, sermons, and preaching. One could say of him, as of Saint
Paul, that he suffered many perils for the salvation of souls and the defense of
the holy church.

He profited the holy church not only with his preaching but also with his
holy writings, beginning with us. For as long as he remained in this city, after
he had enclosed our convent, he wrote and annotated the books for singing
the office throughout the year, the gradual of the saints, and one of the large
psalters; and after he was banished, upon hearing of our troubles, he wrote us
many letters of consolation and helpful instruction, which have all been re-
copied to form a book.[37] Even as he traveled throughout the world preaching
and converting many people, he never forgot about us. He wrote a book called
the *Itinerario* because he went wandering around the world and, wishing to
comfort us and his other friends but being unable to return to Venice until his
period of exile expired, he wrote this book that contains an exposition of the
Song of Songs so marvelously lucid that there is no mind so foggy that it
wouldn't be enlightened by reading it. He also wrote on Genesis, drawing a

36. In 1393, in recognition of his work to reform the Dominican order, Raymond of Capua
named Giovanni vicar general of all the Observant Dominican houses in Italy. On the reform
movement that sprang from his efforts, see Venturino Alce, "La riforma dell'ordine domenicano
nel '400 e nel '500 veneto," in *Riforma della chiesa, cultura e spiritualità nel Quattrocento veneto*, ed.
Giovanni B. Francesco Trolese (Cesena: Badia di Santa Maria del Monte, 1984), 333–43, and, for
the broader movement of reform, Mario Fois, "I religiosi: Decadenza e fermenti innovatori," in *La
chiesa di Venezia tra medioevo ed età moderna*, ed. Giovanni Vian, Contributi alla Storia della Chiesa
Veneziana 3 (Venice: Edizioni Studium Cattolico Veneziano, 1989), 147–82.

37. These letters form the core of Dominici, *Lettere spirituali*. On Giovanni's literary production, including the other works mentioned here, see Thomas Kaeppeli, *Scriptores ordinis praedicatorum medii
aevi*, vol. 2 (Rome: S. Sabinae, 1975), 406–13.

parallel between this convent and Noah's ark. He wrote an exposition of the *Magnificat* and a book on the perfection of charity, and another book on the seven beatitudes; all the aforesaid books are in this convent. Such a lot of lovely sermons and treatises against heresy and the papal schism and in defense of the holy Catholic faith! There is no way I could recount all that this holy man labored to do for the honor of God and for the holy church *usque ad mortem.*

OF THE LEARNING AND VIRTUES OF THIS HOLY FATHER

This holy man was of such sobriety and humility that I am totally inadequate to the task of describing his virtues. However, I do not want to take refuge in my inadequacy and so will speak as best I know how. His venerable mother told me that he was sixteen years old when he entered the order, and he lived to be sixty-five without ever being heard to say an idle word or do a dissolute act. He was always sober and proper in his speech, his movements, and his glances: he was so reserved even toward his mother that she called him her prickly son. He loved chastity and virginity so much that he could never be sated with preaching about and praising this virtue, with the result that many young men and women who heard those elegant sermons made vows of virginity, some in religious orders and some outside them. He was equally sober about eating, in that he followed his order's rules in all circumstances until he fell ill. He also remained and always wanted to be poor, so that he had nothing of his own. Whoever entered his cell found nothing but books and straw, while all the coins and other alms that might be given to him were turned over to the community. When he was banished from this city, he happened to have only five shillings; and with that sum he walked all the way to Florence.[38] Not long thereafter he was made bishop of Ragusa, and subsequently he was named cardinal—not through simony or money, but on account of his great virtues, since Pope Gregory, knowing him to be a man of great deeds and much learning, was very happy to have him by his side. When this blessed father received these honors, he did not puff himself up pompously but instead humbly maintained a level of poverty consonant with his station in life.

One could also say of his humility that while he was vicar of the friaries that he had brought back to the [regular] observance, he was the first to rouse the friars to action when it was time to knead the bread; and when wood or wine or stones or mortar arrived for the work being done on the friary, he was the first to heft it on his shoulders and so set an example for the other friars to

38. On Giovanni's expulsion from Venice, see chronicle, chapter, 9.

follow. He would get up and sweep the friary while everyone was sleeping; when the friars woke up, they would marvel to find it swept and dusted. There were those who noted and kept in mind how he himself behaved, and so the good shepherd taught his flock.

He was also much given to vigils and prayers and devotion. That holy man never remained idle: he meditated, prayed, and studied the Holy Scriptures or wrote, annotated, and illuminated. He was always thinking up more things to do so as not to remain idle. Every day he would say the first mass, since he was kept so busy with preaching, hearing confession, and offering advice; and his masses were always accompanied with tears. He had the gift of prophecy. When some troubled or tempted person asked for his prayers, with great compassion he placed his hands on that person's head, saying, "Be comforted, for help will soon be with you"; and those hands would seem to carry away all the heart's troubles.

He had great spirit and was always eager to do grand deeds for God. Just as he did great deeds for the order, so he did great deeds and endured great hardships for the holy church during the thirteen years that he was part of its leadership—and for all that, he would say and write that he felt he was accomplishing nothing, and that he hoped to return to the order so that he could preach and do something for love of the Lord God. He did all he could to get permission to return to it, but the holy father held him very dear and would never agree to let him go. And so he finished the course of his life amid good intentions and good deeds and went to receive the reward for his labors.

We believe that he is greatly glorified in that eternal homeland. As a sign that this is true, while one of our sisters was in prayer, praying to the Lord for his soul with many tears, she was rapt in spirit and seemed to see a great light. In that light she saw and recognized the face of this blessed father, which seemed to cast rays like the sun, and the whole church was filled with the faces of little children that hovered in the air around this light. This sister was utterly amazed, and she pondered to herself, saying, "My Lord, what do all these children signify?" She heard a voice that said to her, "Be of good cheer. You should know that those children are the souls that have been brought back into the bosom of the holy church by his preaching and his advice, and that is why you see him in such glory." She gazed upon that face and said, "Oh, blessed father, may your daughters be entrusted to your care," and she reported that he laughed as if with pleasure at hearing these words. This sister came to herself very joyous, firmly believing that he enjoyed life eternal and great honor in the sight of the Lord.

Indeed, many things could be said of this holy man and venerable father.

I have recounted only a few of them, since my abilities cannot match what his sanctity deserves; but the little bit that I have written, I have written in order that we not be ungrateful daughters of such a father, and that those who come after us may know who was the founder of this blessed convent, and that in hearing some portion of his virtues they may have an incentive to strive to imitate him, so that with him they might enjoy life eternal *ad quam nos perducat ille qui sine fine vivit et regnat.*[39]

XXXII

HOW SISTER FELICITAS DIED

On August 19, 1423, Sister Felicitas Venier passed from this life. She was a virgin woman who was seventeen years old when she entered the order. She came with great fervor and goodwill and continued in that fashion for seven years. Then she fell sick with a serious illness and received all the holy sacraments, and she serenely departed from this vale of tears. *Deo gratias.*

XXXIII

HOW SISTER PIERA OF CITTÀ DI CASTELLO PASSED FROM THIS LIFE TO THE NEXT

On November 25 of that same year died Sister Piera, a widowed woman who entered the convent at the age of thirty-eight and lived there for twenty-nine years. What, then, should I say of this blessed woman? My tongue is not able to describe her virtues. She was from Città di Castello. She said that even when she was just a little girl she had a good understanding of God; she was married against her will, and she lived with her husband in the fear of God. When she was left a widow, she donned the habit of a penitent of Saint Dominic, to whom she was especially devoted. Having heard of this convent, she came to Venice with our father's permission and encouragement, and with great devotion she entered the convent with our father's permission.

This blessed woman was adorned with all the virtues. She was poor in spirit, and she was satisfied with the barest minimum of temporal goods, without caring about quality. She didn't grumble; she fled idle words; she was very humble and obedient and respectful toward everyone. She had such

39. "To which may he who lives and rules without end lead us."

charity for all that she would have exposed herself to every danger in order to serve them, and they all called her mother. She tended all the sick women and washed all their filth, and she did not abandon them until she saw that they were either dead or out of danger. Thirty sisters died in her hands, and every one of them thought she was in good company with Sister Piera by her side. In short, right up to the very end she never rested from treating everyone alike with charity. One could even say that she died from charity, since when Sister Felicitas was sick with enormous sores and gave off a terrible stench, so that some of the sisters who looked after her were repelled by them, Sister Piera (who was elderly and feeble from illness, and whose limbs all trembled with the force of her feelings for God) still managed to get about the convent and fretted that she could not tend to her when she saw her so covered with sores. One day she went to that sick woman with great fervor and kissed her on the mouth, and then she kissed and cleaned every sore on that body; and as a result the blessed woman contracted that disease and came down with a high fever that laid her out for fifteen days.[40] She received all the holy sacraments in full awareness of God and passed from this miserable life to the desired glory for which she had sighed, desiring God's honor and the salvation of humankind.

She was so fixed upon charity for her neighbors and so eager for their salvation that every day she wept over the great affronts given to our Creator. She prayed tearfully for humankind, and when she heard that there was strife in the holy church or other wars, she would not leave her prayers except to eat or sleep, and many was the time she remained all night long in the church weeping and wailing so loudly that she could be heard throughout the convent. She prayed assiduously for all those who asked for her prayers; and when they were troubled or wanted some favor from God, she made a special prayer. She also prophesied the truth on many subjects. She saw many lovely visions, which were not written down on account of our negligence—and if they had all been recorded in writing they would have made a large book. Of the many things that could be said about this holy woman, I have said little because of my own inadequacies. In brief, she was adorned with many virtues, and one could not see even the slightest defect in her. *Deo gratias.*

---

40. This echoes the famous stories of how Saint Francis of Assisi embraced a leper and (more proximately) how Saint Catherine of Siena drank the foul, pus-filled water that had washed a woman's ulcerated sore. The latter episode was recounted in a text well known in this particular circle of Observant Dominicans: Raymond of Capua's biography of Catherine of Siena (part 2, chap. 4, par. 162). See Raymond of Capua, *The Life of Catherine of Siena,* trans. Conleth Kearns (Dublin: Dominican Publications, 1980), 155.

XXXIV

HOW SISTER ONESTA DEI MARCHESI DIED

In that year, just ten days after Sister Piera—that is, on December 4—Sister Onesta passed from this life. She was the daughter of the marquis of Monte Santa Maria, and thus a woman from a great lineage, very elegant and notoriously worldly. Our father Brother Giovanni Dominici and Brother Giovanni Benedetto (who is at present bishop of Treviso) went to Città di Castello, and while Brother Giovanni was preaching there, this woman, hearing that he was a youth of eighteen, went to his sermon almost as a joke.[41] The Holy Spirit made him speak so effectively that she was converted on the spot; and hearing of this convent, she begged our father and Brother Giovanni to receive her and make arrangements with her brothers to have her sent to Venice. When our father heard her good intentions, he went to see her brothers. There were five or six of them, all great lords who held castles; and when they heard that this sister of theirs had converted, they had a good laugh, saying that she was so worldly and so vivacious that this could never last. The oldest of the brothers, who was a spiritual son of our father, said that he wanted to observe her for several months, and that if she persisted he would send her to Venice. Thus our father and Brother Giovanni returned to Venice while she remained behind, persevering in her good intentions; and she did so well that shortly thereafter one of her brothers accompanied her to Venice together with Sister Piera and Sister Tommasa. She was a widow, twenty-three years old.

Once she had entered the convent, God's grace entered her and she became so conscious of her sins that day and night she lamented the period of her vanities. She likewise afflicted her body, wearing a hair shirt for a long time and fasting and keeping vigil with very great prayers and tears. When she received Communion, she wept with so many tears and sighs that she seemed about to burst. Sometimes I asked her what she was feeling; she replied that she felt such sweetness at God's mercy, who humbled himself to come to so great a sinner as she had been, that she would have burst had she not cried out. And thus she remained in great fervor, caring nothing for her family or for worldly honors. She did the cooking for as long as she could, and she tended the sick and performed many demeaning chores; she served the sisters with great charity and held herself in such contempt that she seemed to retain no

41. On Giovanni Benedetto, bishop of Treviso 1418–37, see Luigi Pesce, *La chiesa di Treviso nel primo Quattrocento*, Italia Sacra 37–39 (Rome: Herder, 1987), 230–85.

memory of her former condition. She even told me that she wanted to go mad in order to wreak vengeance on her body for having so offended its Creator. The Lord granted her wish, so that for several years she bore many stinking sores with great patience. In the end, when Sister Piera died, she had been confined to bed with a fever for ten days. When she heard that Sister Piera had passed away, she wept for the sweet charity she had borne for her and said, "Now my life is done, since when we set out to come here, we promised that we would never abandon each other in life or in death." And so she died ten days after Sister Piera. Many things could be written about this blessed woman, which I omit for the sake of brevity. May the Lord Jesus Christ make us worthy of seeing her in his glory. Amen.

XXXV

HOW SISTER CATERUZZA STELLA DIED

On April 18, 1425, Cateruzza Stella passed from this life. She was a widow and was fifty years old when she entered the order. She was one of the women who entered on the first day that the convent was enclosed, and she lived for another thirty years, eleven months, and eighteen days. This blessed woman was full of prayers and tender feelings for God, and she never remained idle. She was always working or laboring for the common good of the convent, and she often would say, "The good that awaits me is so great that every ache and effort is a pleasure for me." And so she ended her life amid good works and holy desires and received all the holy sacraments with great devotion. The day before she died, she wanted all the sisters to sing hymns for her; and during this singing there came a moment when she seemed to expire and then returned to herself. The prioress asked her if she felt ready to depart; she replied with her face joyous and her hands joined together, "Would that it were already the day in which I might go to my Lord!" And all by herself she crossed herself, saying, "Mary mother of grace," and so in good spirits she went to her benign creator. *Deo gratias.*

XXXVI

HOW SISTER H., A WIDOWED WOMAN, DIED

On December 24 of the aforesaid year Sister H. passed from this life. She was a widowed woman and entered the convent at the age of forty-two and lived there for thirty-one years. She was a lay sister and lived in holy fashion, in great prayer and meditation; in particular, she contemplated the Passion with many moans and sighs. She remained sick for a long time with great patience. Coming to her very end, she recognized that she was dying and said the *Credo* with the sisters, and at the end said, "Sisters, set up the candles, because I am departing."[42] All at once she rolled her eyes and expired, fully armed with all the holy sacraments.

XXXVII

HOW SISTER MARINA PISANI PASSED FROM THIS LIFE

On May 18, 1426, Sister Marina Pisani passed from this life. She remained a widow for fifteen years and then, not wishing to mix any more in the world, took Jesus Christ to be her spouse. Dedicating herself to prayer and fasting and many good works, she visited the poor, the sick, and prisoners and served the Lord. When this convent was built she entered inside it, and she was one of those women who entered the first day. She was forty years old when she entered, and she lived for thirty years and eleven months in the convent. She remained sick for a long time with good patience. When she reached her very end, she received all the holy sacraments very devoutly and went to the Lord.

XXXVIII

HOW SISTER BERUZZA ZIROLDI DIED

On November 4 of that same year Sister Beruzza Ziroldi passed from this life. She was left a widow at the age of thirteen; wanting nothing more to do with the world, she became a nun at San Girolamo and lived there in a holy manner. The yearning to live the common life grew in her, so she came here and was received with five women nine days after the convent was enclosed; she was twenty-five years old and lived here for thirty-two years and five months.[43] This blessed woman had a sweet character and was very devoted

---

42. Recital of the creed was recommended for laypeople in fifteenth-century devotional hand-books such as the *Libretto della dottrina cristiana attribuito a S. Antonino arcivescovo di Firenze*, ed. Gilberto Aranci (Florence: Angelo Pontecorboli Editore, 1996), 22–28.

43. The chronicle, chapter 5, says there were seven of them and gives Beruzza Ziroldi's age as thirty—which, like the age of twenty-five given here, should be taken as an approximation. I have standardized the spelling of her name, preferring that of the chronicle to the way it is spelled here in the necrology: Ciriuola.

to the Passion of Christ: from Holy Thursday until Easter Sunday she would
never take any food other than the Holy Communion. She was filled with
love of God and charity for her neighbor. When the time of her death approached, she fell ill with dropsy, with which she lay ill for seven months
with great patience, always praising God. She devoutly received all the holy
sacraments and on the night that she died, the sisters asked if she wanted
anything; she replied with great fervor and with her arms thrown wide, "I
want God's grace." Having said this, *inclinavit chapite, emisit spiritum* and went to
her Lord.[44]

XXXIX

HOW SISTER ORSA FRAGANESI DIED

On the twenty-first of that month Sister Orsa Fraganesi passed from this life.
This lady was a nun at San Girolamo and came with Sister Beruzza; just as they
loved and accompanied one another in life, so they were not separated even in
death. This woman was a virgin and came here with great fervor and lived for
thirty-two years and five and a half months. She was most observant and did
great penitence for as long as she could, and she loved holy poverty and the
community very much. She remained ill with consumption for a long time.
When she reached her very end, she received all the holy sacraments and
rested in peace. Amen.

XL

HOW SISTER ZANETTA DALLE BOCCOLE DIED

On April 23, 1427, Sister Zanetta dalle Boccole passed from this life. She was
a widow; she was twenty-two years old when she converted, and with great
fervor she left two children to God's keeping and entered as a nun here inside,
where she lived for thirty-two years and four months. She was healthy and
strong and labored willingly right up to the end, but one and a half months before her death she discovered that she had a cancer on her right breast that
caused much pain and terrible sores, so that all the sisters grieved with compassion. With great patience she called unceasingly on God and the Madonna
with all the saints to aid her, so that she could believe firmly that God and the
Madonna with all the saints would help her and free her from so much suffer-

44. John 19:30: "He bowed his head and gave up his spirit."

ing. Indeed, our Lord said, "Whoever calls upon me, I will hear him and free him and glorify him." In confirmation of this, a few days before she expired one of the sisters saw in a dream many male and female saints near the infirmary, who said, "We have come to accompany Sister Zanetta because she invoked us so much." And she seemed to see Sister Zanetta rise from bed hale and hearty and go off in the company of those saints. Another of the women who tended her saw in a dream that she grew wings and flew from the bed. For this reason we may think that she numbers among the blessed, since the crown is promised to whoever fights faithfully.

XLI

HOW SISTER BENEDETTA ROSSO DIED

On August 8 of that year Sister Benedetta Rosso passed from this life. She entered this convent at the age of ten and lived for twenty-seven years, for twenty-three years of which she remained sick with a very serious illness. For a long time she had severe tremors; then she became consumptive and often spit up gobs of blood, and she frequently received Communion in bed thinking she was about to die. She had great devotion to the holy sacrament of Christ's body. One time when she was gushing blood and feared she would die, she asked for and received the sacrament with great devotion, and by virtue of the sacrament the bleeding stopped immediately. As sick as she was, whenever she could walk, she would often be found praying in the church or doing good works. She ended her life in this fashion: when there was a great pestilence in this city, the Lord saw fit that we too would share in this scourge, and he started with this Sister Benedetta, who received all the holy sacraments most devoutly and passed to her dearly beloved spouse. *Deo gratias.*

XLII

HOW SISTER CECILIA DIED

On the seventeenth of that month Sister Cecilia Dotto dalla Dieta passed from this life. She was a virgin and entered the convent the first day it was enclosed; she was then eighteen years old, and she lived here for thirty-three years.[45] She was a good nun, very obedient, and she was healthy and vigorous.

---

45. In an evident error, the text says she lived in the convent for twenty-three years.

When the pestilence struck her she received all the holy sacraments and passed away peacefully. *Deo gratias.*

XLIII

HOW SISTER TOMMASA OF CITTÀ DI CASTELLO DIED

In 1428 Sister Tommasa of Città di Castello passed from this life. She was a virgin who entered the convent with Sister Piera and Sister Onesta at the age of nineteen and lived for thirty-three years and six months. She was a woman of great prayer, very charitable and obliging to all. A cancerous disease struck her and devoured half her foot. She lived with this harsh ailment for three months, blessing the Lord constantly, and so with great patience she finished in peace with all the holy sacraments.

XLIV

HOW SISTER ELENA RIDOLFI DIED

In 1429 Sister Elena Ridolfi passed from this mortal life. She entered here as a forty-year-old widow and lived in the convent for thirty-five years. While she was still with her husband, she was converted with great fervor by our father's sermons. She gave herself to prayer and fasting, wearing a hair shirt and doing many other penances; after she was widowed, she would feed seven poor persons before eating herself. Once she had entered the convent, she strove to observe the rule to perfection, bearing herself humbly and patiently. It pleased the Lord to grant her rest, sending her a disease of the throat, and she soon left this mortal life and went to the eternal one—to which may our Lord Jesus Christ guide us. Amen.

XLV

HOW SISTER MARIA PALAZZI DIED

In 1431 Sister Maria Palazzi passed from this life on March 4. She entered on the first day that the convent was enclosed and was vested as a lay sister. She was then twenty-two years old, and she lived here in the convent for thirty-six years and eight months. She entered with great fervor and lived virtuously, and having received all the holy sacraments with good effect she passed from this life to the eternal one. *Deo gratias.*

XLVI

HOW SISTER GERONIMA DEI CANCELLIERI DIED

On the tenth of that month Sister Geronima dei Cancellieri passed from this miserable life. She was a widow who entered the convent at the age of fifty-one and lived here for twenty-six years. This woman was the daughter of the count of Pistoia; all her brothers were counts and of high estate.[46] She married a knight and was left a widow while still young, and she had always had a desire to serve God. She had always longed to go someplace where she was neither known nor honored. As it pleased God, who grants good wishes, she was converted by the sermons of our father, who at that time was preaching in Tuscany; and upon hearing of the good reputation of this convent, she arranged with him to come to Venice. When this reached the ears of her two sons, who were highly respected knights, and her two married daughters, they sent word to all the passes as far as Rimini to have her detained. As it pleased God, she got by them all and came to incarcerate herself in here for his love. How she bore herself humbly and virtuously would make a long tale. She performed all the duties with great humility and with great charity, and she was always the first to respond, both day and night, to all the needs of the sisters, healthy and ill. She always warmed the syrups for all the women and performed many other chores. When the prioress died, we chose this woman as prioress, and she lived for ten years as prioress.[47] She behaved not like a prioress but like a servant to all. She followed the religious life to perfection until she fell ill with a very serious infirmity, and she lived for nine years with the utmost patience until she serenely rendered her soul to her sweet creator.

XLVII

HOW SISTER EUFRASIA MINIO DIED

On the last day of June in 1432, Sister Eufrasia Minio passed from this life. She was a virgin who entered the convent at the age of seven and lived laudably as a good nun for thirty-five years. She fell ill with wasting fever and consump-

46. The Cancellieri were one of the chief families of Pistoia and for centuries had played a leading role in the factional strife that troubled that city. On the Cancellieri as the source of the divisions that led to Dante's exile from Florence, see *Dino Compagni's Chronicle of Florence*, trans. Daniel E. Bornstein (Philadelphia: University of Pennsylvania Press, 1986), 28–30. On the leading members of the family and the composition of their faction in the early fifteenth century, see Luca Dominici, *Cronache*, vol. 2, *Cronaca seconda*, ed. Giovan Carlo Gigliotti (Pistoia: Alberto Pacinotti, 1939), 13–19.

47. Since the first prioress, Sister Lucia Tiepolo, died in 1413, this would place Sister Geronima's term in office as 1413 to 1422–23.

tion, and she bore this illness for eighteen years with tremendous suffering: never was there seen such thinness as in that body. She bore her infirmity with the greatest patience. Finally, having received all the most holy sacraments, gazing upon the crucifix and crossing her hands over her breast, she serenely rendered her soul to her dear spouse Lord Jesus Christ. Amen.

XLVIII

HOW SISTER ISABETTA TOMMASINI DIED

In 1433 Sister Isabetta Tommasini, who was a virgin, passed from this life. At the beginning of this book I told of the origins of her conversion and of how God made her the founder of this convent. She entered at the age of sixteen and lived here for thirty-seven years, nine months, and seven days. My tongue could not tell how exemplary was her life and how full of good works. She was learned in the Holy Scripture; when she had to sermonize in chapter she seemed like a doctor [of theology]. She was likewise a source of good counsel: many troubled men, both religious and secular, and many women came to her, and all went away consoled. This holy woman was purest in mind and body, devout, very humble, gentle, and kind, lowly in dress, and in all her deeds she set a good example. Our father made her first subprioress, but because she was too young, the older women ran things. But she stayed in that office for a short time and humbly remained respectful and obedient to all the officials. When she was forty-three years old she was named prioress by general agreement of all the sisters, and she held that office for ten years, nine months, and seven days. She conducted herself very prudently, zealous for the honor of God and the peace and unity of the sisters, and respectful toward all the sisters. When it pleased God to grant her rest, she came down with a high fever that lasted thirteen days, and she received all the holy sacraments very devoutly. As her death approached she urged the sisters to conduct themselves well, saying to them, "Dear daughters, we have such a good Lord that we need not fear going to him. I am going to my wedding; hec est requies mea in seculum seculi," and many other lovely words.[48] Then she said, "I am stripped of myself and throw myself entirely on him; may my Lord do with me as he pleases." She continued in good meditation; her speech and face were so tranquil that she seemed to have no fear of death, and the last words that she said were, "Ibo in civitatem sanctam Syon."[49] She drew herself up straight with her face tranquil, and in a few

48. Ps. 132:14: "This is my resting place for ever; here I will dwell, for I have desired it."
49. "I shall go to the holy city of Zion."

moments she expired, so that considering her good life and her happy demise, I believe she is in paradise. As evidence that this is true, one of the sisters who looked after her went to her cell that evening to rest and did not hear the clapper, and when the bell was sounded she ran, saying, "Alas, I didn't hear the clapper and so didn't witness the passing of my dear mother, but the Lord Jesus Christ showed her to me while sleeping." She said that she saw two venerable gentlemen enter the cell where she lay, go to the bed, and take her by the hand and say, "Come with me to the homeland." A young laywoman saw something similar in her own home. In her sleep, she saw her go accompanied by two gentlemen and enter a beautiful garden, and when she woke up she said, "The prioress of Corpus Domini must have passed from this life." Other sisters, too, saw her doing very well, and this I believe by the grace of God, who I pray may make us worthy of imitating her virtues.

XLIX

HOW SISTER MARIA TASSO DIED

In 1436 Sister Maria Tasso passed from this life on the last day of March. She entered on the first day that the convent was enclosed; she was thirty-five years old, and she lived here for thirty-nine years and nine months.[50] She was very virtuous and proper. While still a young woman, she despised the world and served God with great humility. She very devoutly went to visit the holy sepulcher and all the sacred places of Rome, and then she came to seal herself in Christ's side.[51] I am not capable of recounting how religiously and virtuously she comported herself and with what purity, humility, and charity; no one could tell how fervently and tearfully she prayed. Finally she became dropsied, and for three years she remained parched and mute with the greatest patience. In the end, with us gathered around her singing psalms, her face brightened and within three breaths she expired. *Deo gratias.*

---

50. The year given in the text may be an error for 1434; if not, the time spent in the convent is off by two years.

51. This is the only mention of pilgrimage in the necrology, but Sister Maria Tasso was certainly not the only woman to undertake these devotional journeys. Her English contemporary Margery Kempe made pilgrimages to the very places mentioned here—Rome and the Holy Land—in 1413–15.

BIBLIOGRAPHY

PRIMARY SOURCES

Alberti, Leon Battista (1404–72). *The Family in Renaissance Florence.* Trans. Renée Neu Watkins. Columbia: University of South Carolina Press, 1969.

Ariosto, Ludovico (1474–1533). *Orlando Furioso.* Trans. Barbara Reynolds. 2 vols. New York: Penguin Books, 1975, 1977.

Astell, Mary (1666–1731). *The First English Feminist: Reflections on Marriage and Other Writings.* Ed. and introd. Bridget Hill. New York: St. Martin's Press, 1986.

Barbaro, Francesco (1390–1454). *On Wifely Duties.* Trans. Benjamin Kohl. In *The Earthly Republic,* ed. Benjamin Kohl and R. G. Witt, 179–228. Philadelphia: University of Pennsylvania Press, 1978, Translation of preface and book 2.

Boccaccio, Giovanni (1313–75). *Concerning Famous Women.* Trans. Guido A. Guarino. New Brunswick: Rutgers University Press, 1963.

____. *Corbaccio, or The Labyrinth of Love.* Trans. Anthony K. Cassell. 2d rev. ed. Binghamton, N.Y.: Medieval and Renaissance Texts and Studies, 1993.

Bruni, Leonardo (1370–1444). "On the Study of Literature (1405) to Lady Battista Malatesta of Moltefeltro." In *The Humanism of Leonardo Bruni: Selected Texts,* trans. and introd. Gordon Griffiths, James Hankins, and David Thompson, 240–51. Binghamton, N.Y.: Medieval and Renaissance Studies and Texts, 1987.

Castiglione, Baldassare (1478–1529). *The Book of the Courtier.* Trans. George Bull. New York: Penguin, 1967.

Dominici, Giovanni. "Iter perusinum." In Giovanni Dominici, *Lettere spirituali,* ed. Maria-Teresa Casella and Giovanni Pozzi, 186–93. Spicilegium Friburgense 13. Freiburg: Edizioni Universitarie, 1969.

————. *Lettere spirituali.* Ed. Maria-Teresa Casella and Giovanni Pozzi. Spicilegium Friburgense 13. Freiburg: Edizioni Universitarie, 1969.

————. *Lucula Noctis.* Ed. Edmund Hunt. Notre Dame: University of Notre Dame Press, 1940.

Elyot, Thomas (1490–1546). *Defence of Good Women: The Feminist Controversy of the Renaissance.* Ed. Diane Bornstein. Facsimile Reproductions. New York: Delmar, 1980.

Erasmus, Desiderius (1467–1536). *Erasmus on Women.* Ed. Erika Rummel. Toronto: University of Toronto Press, 1996.

————. *The Praise of Folly.* Trans. with intro. and commentary Clarence H. Miller. New

Haven: Yale Univesity Press, 1979. Best edition, since it indicates additions to the text between 1511 and 1516.

Facchiano, Annamaria. *Monasteri femminili e nobiltà a Napoli tra medioevo ed età moderna: Il necrologio di S. Patrizia (secc. XII–XVI).* Fonti per la Storia del Mezzogiorno Medievale 11. Altavilla Silentina (Salerno): Edizioni Studi Storici Meridionali, 1992.

Kempe, Margery (1373–1439). *The Book of Margery Kempe.* Trans. Barry Windeatt. New York: Viking Penguin, 1986.

King, Margaret L., and Albert Rabil Jr., eds. *Her Immaculate Hand: Selected Works by and about the Women Humanists of Quattrocento Italy.* Binghamton, N.Y.: Medieval and Renaissance Texts and Studies, 1983; 2d rev.paperback ed., 1991.

Klein, Joan Larsen, ed. *Daughters, Wives, and Widows: Writings by Men about Women and Marriage in England, 1500–1640.* Urbana: University of Illinois Press, 1992.

Knox, John (1505–72). *The Political Writings of John Knox: The First Blast of the Trumpet against the Monstrous Regiment of Women and Other Selected Works.* Ed. Marvin A. Breslow. Washington, D.C.: Folger Shakespeare Library, 1985.

Kors, Alan C., and Edward Peters, eds. *Witchcraft in Europe, 1100–1700: A Documentary History.* Philadelphia: University of Pennsylvania Press, 1972.

Krämer, Heinrich, and Jacob Sprenger. *Malleus Maleficarum* (ca. 1487). Trans. Montague Summers. London: Pushkin Press, 1928; reprinted New York: Dover, 1971. The "Hammer of Witches" was a convenient source for all the misogynistic commonplaces on the eve of the sixteenth century and an important text in the witch craze of the following centuries.

Libretto della dottrina cristiana attribuito a S. Antonio arcivescovo di Firenze. Ed. Gilberto Aranci. Florence: Angelo Pontecorboli Editore, 1996.

Lorris, William de, and Jean de Meun. *The Romance of the Rose.* Trans. Charles Dahlbert. Princeton: Princeton University Press, 1971; reprinted Hanover, N.H.: University Press of New England, 1983.

Marguerite d'Angoulême, queen of Navarre (1492–1549). *The Heptameron.* Trans. P. A. Chilton. New York: Viking Penguin, 1984.

Medioli, Francesca, ed. *L'"Inferno monacale" di Arcangela Tarabotti.* Turin: Rosenberg e Sellier, 1990.

Memoriale di Monteluce: Cronaca del monastero delle Clarisse di Perugia dal 1448 al 1838. Ed. Chiara Agusta Laniati, intro. Ugolino Nicolini. Assisi: Porziuncola, 1983.

Orlandi, Stefano. *Necrologio di S. Maria Novella, 1235–1504.* Florence: Olschki, 1955.

Pizan, Christine de (1365–1431). *The Book of the City of Ladies.* Trans. Earl Jeffrey Richards, foreword Marina Warner. New York: Persea Books, 1982.

————. *The Treasure of the City of Ladies.* Trans. Sarah Lawson. New York: Viking Penguin, 1985. Also trans. and introd. Charity Cannon Willard, ed. and introd. Madeleine P. Cosman. New York: Persea Books, 1989.

Il Processo Castellano. Ed. Marie-Hyacinthe Laurent. Fontes Vitae S. Catharinae Senensis Historici 9. Milan: Fratelli Bocca, 1942.

Raymond of Capua. *The Life of Catherine of Siena.* Trans. Conleth Kearns. Dublin: Dominican Publications, 1980.

Riccoboni, Bartolomea. *Cronaca del Corpus Domini.* In Giovanni Dominici, *Lettere spirituali,* ed. Maria-Teresa Casella and Giovanni Pozzi, 257–94. Spicilegium Friburgense 13. Freiburg: Edizioni Universitarie, 1969.

————. *Necrologio del Corpus Domini.* In Giovanni Dominici, *Lettere spirituali,* ed. Maria-

Teresa Casella and Giovanni Pozzi, 295–330. Spicilegium Friburgense 13. Freiburg: Edizioni Universitarie, 1969.

Ricordanze del monastero di S. Lucia o.s.c. in Foligno (cronache 1424–1786). Ed. Angela Emmanuela Scandella with an appendix by Giovanni Boccali. Assisi: Porziuncola, 1987.

Spenser, Edmund (1552–99). *The Faerie Queene*. Ed. Thomas P. Roche Jr. with the assistance of C. Patrick O'Donnell Jr. New Haven: Yale University Press, 1978.

Tarabotti, Arcangela. *Paternal Tyranny*. Trans. Letizia Panizza. Chicago: University of Chicago Press, forthcoming.

———. [Galerana Baratotti]. *La semplicità ingannata*. Leiden, 1654.

Teresa of Avila (1515–82). *The Life of Saint Teresa of Avila by Herself*. Trans. J. M. Cohen. New York: Viking Penguin, 1957.

Tugwell, Simon, ed. and trans. *Early Dominicans: Selected Writings*. New York: Paulist Press, 1982.

Vives, Juan Luis (1492–1540). *The Instruction of the Christian Woman*. Trans. Rycharde Hyrde. London, 1524, 1557.

Weyer, Johann (1515–88). *Witches, Devils, and Doctors in the Renaissance: Johann Weyer, "De praestigiis daemonum."* Ed. George Mora with Benjamin G. Kohl, Erik Midelfort, and Helen Bacon, trans. John Shea. Binghamton, N.Y.: Medieval and Renaissance Texts and Studies, 1991.

Wilson, Katharina M., ed. *Medieval Women Writers*. Athens: University of Georgia Press, 1984.

———, ed. *Women Writers of the Renaissance and Reformation*. Athens: University of Georgia Press, 1987.

Wilson, Katharina M., and Frank J. Warnke, eds. *Women Writers of the Seventeenth Century*. Athens: University of Georgia Press, 1989.

Women Writers in English, 1350–1805. 30 volumes projected. New York: Oxford University Press, 1993–.

SECONDARY SOURCES

Agostini, Giovanni degli. *Notizie istorico-critiche intorno la vita e le opere degli scrittori viniziani*, vol. 1. Venice: Simone Occhi, 1752; reprinted Bologna: Forni, 1975.

Beilin, Elaine V. *Redeeming Eve: Women Writers of the English Renaissance*. Princeton: Princeton University Press, 1987.

Benson, Pamela Joseph. *The Invention of Renaissance Woman: The Challenge of Female Independence in the Literature and Thought of Italy and England*. University Park: Pennsylvania State University Press, 1992.

Bloch, R. Howard. *Medieval Misogyny and the Invention of Western Romantic Love*. Chicago: University of Chicago Press, 1991.

Bornstein, Daniel E. *The Bianchi of 1399: Popular Devotion in Late Medieval Italy*. Ithaca: Cornell University Press, 1993.

———. "Dominican Friar, Lay Saint: The Case of Marcolino of Forlì." *Church History* 66 (1997): 252–67.

———. "Giovanni Dominici, the Bianchi, and Venice: Symbolic Action and Interpretive Grids." *Journal of Medieval and Renaissance Studies* 23 (1993): 143–71.

———. "Spiritual Kinship and Domestic Devotions." In *Gender and Society in Renaissance*

Italy, ed. Judith C. Brown and Robert C. Davis, 173–92. London: Addison Wesley Longman, 1998.

Bornstein, Daniel E., and Roberto Rusconi, eds. *Women and Religion in Medieval and Renaissance Italy.* Chicago: University of Chicago Press, 1996.

Bynum, Caroline Walker. *Fragmentation and Redemption: Essays on Gender and the Human Body in Medieval Europe.* New York: Zone Books, 1991.

———. "Religious Women in the Later Middle Ages." In *Christian Spirituality*, vol. 2, *High Middle Ages and Reformation*, ed. Jill Raitt with Bernard McGinn and John Meyendorff, 121–39. New York: Crossroad, 1987.

Canosa, Romano. *Il velo e il cappuccio: Monacazioni forzate e sessualità nei conventi femminili in Italia tra Quattrocento e Settecento.* Rome, 1991.

Casella, Maria Teresa, and Giovanni Pozzi. "Giunta al Dominici." *Italia Medioevale e Umanistica* 14 (1971): 131–91.

Chojnacki, Stanley. "In Search of the Venetian Patriciate: Families and Factions in the Fourteenth Century." In *Renaissance Venice*, ed. J. R. Hale, 47–90. London: Faber and Faber, 1973.

Clark, Elizabeth A. *Ascetic Piety and Women's Faith: Essays on Late Ancient Christianity.* Lewiston, N.Y.: Edwin Mellen, 1986.

Cracco, Giorgio. "La spiritualità italiana del Tre-Quattrocento: Linee interpretative." *Studia Patavina* 18 (1971): 74–116.

Davis, Natalie Zemon. *Society and Culture in Early Modern France.* Stanford: Stanford University Press, 1975. See especially chapters 3 and 5.

Dean, Trevor, and K. J. P. Lowe, eds. *Marriage in Renaissance Italy.* Cambridge: Cambridge University Press, 1997.

Dixon, Suzanne. *The Roman Family.* Baltimore: Johns Hopkins University Press, 1992.

Dobrowolski, Pawel. "Piety and Death in Venice: A Reading of the Fifteenth-Century Chronicle and the Necrology of Corpus Domini." *Bullettino dell'Istituto Storico Italiano per il Medio Evo* 92 (1985–86): 295–324.

Ferguson, Margaret W., Maureen Quilligan, and Nancy J. Vickers, eds. *Rewriting the Renaissance: The Discourses of Sexual Difference in Early Modern Europe.* Chicago: University of Chicago Press, 1987.

Gardner, Jane F. *Women in Roman Law and Society.* Bloomington: Indiana University Press, 1986.

Girgensohn, Dieter. *Kirche, Politik und adelige Regierung in der Republik Venedig zu Beginn des 15. Jahrhunderts.* Göttingen: Vandenhoek und Ruprecht, 1996.

———. *Venezia e il primo veneziano sulla cattedra di S. Pietro: Gregorio XII (Angelo Correr), 1406–1415,* Centro Tedesco di Studi Veneziani, Quaderni 30. Venice: Centro Tedesco di Studi Veneziani, 1985.

Harvey, Barbara. *Living and Dying in England, 1100–1540: The Monastic Experience.* Oxford: Oxford University Press, 1993.

Herlihy, David. "Did Women Have a Renaissance? A Reconsideration." *Medievalia et Humanistica*, n.s. 13 (1985): 1–22.

A History of Women in the West. Vol. 1. *From Ancient Goddesses to Christian Saints.* Ed. Pauline Schmitt Pantel. Cambridge: Harvard University Press, 1992.

A History of Women in the West. Vol. 2. *Silences of the Middle Ages.* Ed. Christiane Klapisch-Zuber. Cambridge: Harvard University Press, 1992.

A History of Women in the West. Vol. 3. *Renaissance and Enlightenment Paradoxes.* Ed. Natalie Zemon Davis and Arlette Farge. Cambridge: Harvard University Press, 1993.

Horowitz, Maryanne Cline. "Aristotle and Women." *Journal of the History of Biology* 9 (1976): 183–213.

Hull, Suzanne W. *Chaste, Silent, and Obedient: English Books for Women, 1475–1640.* San Marino, Calif.: Huntington Library, 1982.

Jordan, Constance. *Renaissance Feminism: Literary Texts and Political Models.* Ithaca: Cornell University Press, 1990.

Kelly, Joan. "Did Women Have a Renaissance?" In her *Women, History, and Theory,* 19–50. Chicago: University of Chicago Press, 1984. Also in *Becoming Visible: Women in European History,* ed. Renate Bridenthal, Claudia Koonz, and Susan M. Stuard, 2d ed., 175–202. Boston: Houghton Mifflin, 1987.

———. "Early Feminist Theory and the *Querelle des Femmes.*" In her *Women, History, and Theory,* 65–109. Chicago: University of Chicago Press, 1984.

Kelso, Ruth. *Doctrine for the Lady of the Renaissance.* Foreword by Katharine M. Rogers. Urbana: University of Illinois Press, 1956, 1978.

Kieckhefer, Richard. "Major Currents in Late Medieval Devotion." In *Christian Spirituality,* vol. 2, *High Middle Ages and Reformation,* ed. Jill Raitt with Bernard McGinn and John Meyendorff, 75–108. New York: Crossroad, 1987.

King, Margaret L. "Caldiera and the Barbaros on Marriage and the Family: Humanist Reflections of Venetian Realities." *Journal of Medieval and Renaissance Studies* 6 (1976): 19–50.

Kirshner, Julius, and Anthony Molho. "The Dowry Fund and the Marriage Market in Early Quattrocento Florence." *Journal of Modern History* 50 (1978): 403–38.

Laqueur, Thomas. *Making Sex: Body and Gender from the Greeks to Freud.* Cambridge: Harvard University Press, 1990.

Lerner, Gerda. *Creation of Feminist Consciousness, 1000–1870.* New York: Oxford University Press, 1994.

Landi, Aldo. *Il papa deposto (Pisa 1409): L'idea conciliare nel grande scisma.* Turin: Claudiana, 1985.

Lewis, Gertrude Jaron. *By Women, for Women, about Women: The Sister-Books of Fourteenth Century Germany.* Toronto: Pontifical Institute of Mediaeval Studies, 1996.

Lochrie, Karma. *Margery Kempe and Translations of the Flesh.* Philadelphia: University of Pennsylvania Press, 1992.

Maclean, Ian. *The Renaissance Notion of Women: A Study of the Fortunes of Scholasticism and Medical Science in European Intellectual Life.* Cambridge: Cambridge University Press, 1980.

———. *Woman Triumphant: Feminism in French Literature, 1610–1652.* Oxford: Clarendon Press, 1977.

Matter, E. Ann, and John Coakley, eds. *Creative Women in Medieval and Early Modern Italy: A Religious and Artistic Renaissance.* Philadelphia: University of Pennsylvania Press, 1994.

Molho, Anthony. *Marriage Alliance in Late Medieval Florence.* Cambridge: Harvard University Press, 1994.

Monson, Craig A., ed. *The Crannied Wall: Women, Religion, and the Arts in Early Modern Europe.* Ann Arbor: University of Michigan Press, 1992.

Muir, Edward. *Civic Ritual in Renaissance Venice.* Princeton: Princeton University Press, 1981.

Oakley, Francis. *The Western Church in the Later Middle Ages.* Ithaca: Cornell University Press, 1979.

Okin, Susan Moller. *Women in Western Political Thought.* Princeton: Princeton University Press, 1979.

Origo, Iris. *The World of San Bernardino.* New York: Harcourt, Brace and World, 1962.

Pagels, Elaine. *Adam, Eve, and the Serpent.* New York: HarperCollins, 1988.

Pomeroy, Sarah B. *Goddesses, Whores, Wives, and Slaves: Women in Classical Antiquity.* New York: Schocken Books, 1976.

Rose, Mary Beth, ed. *Women in the Middle Ages and the Renaissance: Literary and Historical Perspectives.* Syracuse: Syracuse University Press, 1986.

Rubin, Miri. *Corpus Christi: The Eucharist in Late Medieval Culture.* Cambridge: Cambridge University Press, 1991.

Rusconi, Roberto. *L'attesa della fine: Crisi della società, profezia ed apocalisse in Italia al tempo del grande scisma d'Occidente (1378–1417).* Rome: Istituto Storico Italiano per il Medio Evo, 1979.

Sbriziolo, Lia. "Note su Giovanni Dominici, I: La 'spiritualità' del Dominici nelle lettere alle suore veneziane del Corpus Christi." *Rivista di Storia della Chiesa in Italia* 24 (1970): 4–30.

Sommerville, Margaret R. *Sex and Subjection: Attitudes to Women in Early-Modern Society.* London: Arnold, 1995.

Stuard, Susan M. "The Dominion of Gender: Women's Fortunes in the High Middle Ages." In *Becoming Visible: Women in European History,* ed. Renate Bridenthal, Claudia Koonz, and Susan M. Stuard, 153–72. 2d ed. Boston: Houghton Mifflin, 1987.

Swanson, R. N. *Religion and Devotion in Europe, c. 1215–c. 1515.* Cambridge: Cambridge University Press, 1995.

Tetel, Marcel. *Marguerite de Navarre's "Heptameron": Themes, Language, and Structure.* Durham, N.C.: Duke University Press, 1973.

Tierney, Brian. *Foundations of the Conciliar Theory.* Cambridge: Cambridge University Press, 1955.

Treggiari, Susan. *Roman Marriage: Iusti Coniuges from the Time of Cicero to the Time of Ulpian.* Oxford: Oxford University Press, 1991.

Trolese, Giovanni B. Francesco, ed. *Riforma della chiesa, cultura e spiritualità nel Quattrocento veneto.* Cesena: Badia di Santa Maria del Monte, 1984.

Ullmann, Walter. *The Origins of the Great Schism: A Study in Fourteenth-Century Ecclesiastical History,* 2d ed. Hamden, Conn.: Archon Books, 1972.

Vian, Giovanni, ed. *La chiesa di Venezia tra medioevo ed età moderna.* Contributi alla Storia della Chiesa Veneziana 3. Venice: Edizioni Studium Cattolico Veneziano, 1989.

Walsh, William T. *St. Teresa of Avila: A Biography.* Rockford, Ill.: TAN Books, 1987.

Warner, Marina. *Alone of All Her Sex: The Myth and Cult of the Virgin Mary.* New York: Knopf, 1976.

Weinstein, Donald, and Rudolph M. Bell. *Saints and Society: The Two Worlds of Western Christendom, 1000–1700.* Chicago: University of Chicago Press, 1982.

Wiesner, Merry E. *Women and Gender in Early Modern Europe.* Cambridge: Cambridge University Press, 1993.

Willard, Charity Cannon. *Christine de Pizan: Her Life and Works.* New York: Persea Books, 1984.

Wilson, Katharina, ed. *An Encyclopedia of Continental Women Writers.* New York: Garland, 1991.

Zarri, Gabriella. "Living Saints: A Typology of Female Sanctity in the Early Sixteenth Century." In *Women and Religion in Medieval and Renaissance Italy,* ed. Daniel Bornstein and Roberto Rusconi, 219–303. Chicago: University of Chicago Press, 1996.

INDEX

2 /5—